INTENTIONAL PARENTING

A Guide for Christian Families

Linda Stahnke

Axiom Press, LLC
Colorado Springs, CO

Intentional Parenting. Copyright ©2012 by Linda Stahnke. Manufactured in the United States of America. All rights reserved. No other part of this book may be reproduced in any form or by any electronic or mechanical means including information storage and retrieval systems without permission in writing from the publisher, except by a reviewer, who may quote brief passages in a review. Published by Axiom Press, LLC, 6860 Donnelaith Place, Colorado Springs, CO 80922. (719) 391-1629. First edition.
For more information see www.IntentionalParenting.us

ISBN 978-1-62890-176-4

E-Book ISBN 978-1-62890-177-1

"Scripture quotations taken from the Amplified® Bible, Copyright © 1954, 1958, 1962, 1964, 1965, 1987 by The Lockman Foundation. Used by permission." (www.Lockman.org)

Scripture taken from the HOLY BIBLE, NEW INTERNATIONAL VERSION®. NIV®. Copyright © 1973, 1978, 1984 by International Bible Society. Used by permission of Zondervan. All rights reserved worldwide.

Cover design by Josh Webb   www.JoshWebb.co

Dedication

Dedicated to my husband, George, who always calls me up to a higher level of Christian living. Thank you for challenging me to let our kids learn how to do everything.

Dedicated to our five wonderful children, Jonathan, Kirstie, Melody, Phillip, and Amanda, upon whom we practiced (and practiced) these concepts. Thank you for your patience with our mistakes and for taking all we taught you to the next level.

And dedicated to my friend, Kristina, who asked the questions that started the writing. Your quest to be a godly wife and mother lit the fire under me that I needed and gave shape to this book.

Acknowledgements

Special thanks to my parents who placed the highest priority on seeking God's will for our lives and on loving the Bible.

Special thanks to Radiant Church, Colorado Springs for letting me teach the class that gave form to ideas. Thanks especially to Jenny Green, "admin" extraordinaire.

Special thanks to my friend Thea, mom of *The Sonflowerz*. Your cry for a parenting book gave me the impetus to start writing and keep writing.

Permissions

Character Trait List, pp. 113-115 reprinted by permission, Institute in Basic Life Principles. www.iblp.org.

About the Author

Linda Stahnke has worked as a consultant for nonprofit organizations, writing grants and assisting with strategic planning. She also served as a Development Director for a faith-based nonprofit in Colorado Springs that serves the needy.

She is the founder and former CEO of a public charter school that opened with 325 students and grew to nearly 800 students and two campuses in the four years of her time there. The school was known for its strong character education focus, unique special education programs, and parent involvement. It received several awards for excellence and a 96% parent-satisfaction rating.

Linda worked as an activist and legislative analyst for several educational groups. She reported to and motivated the public through a weekly appearance on a 3-hour live call-in talk show throughout the 90s, emphasizing awareness and involvement of voters in family issues. She co-hosted and interviewed leaders, political candidates and policy makers. During this time the Colorado Springs Gazette named her one of four "Influential Women" in the city. Linda also served on a focus group for PBS' *Newshour with Jim Lehrer,* providing conservative input for 10 years.

Linda and her husband George served on the Board of the Colorado Springs Homeschool Support Group for 9 years, assisting in its growth from 20 families to over 700 families in the Pikes Peak region during the late 1980s and early 1990s. After their last child graduated, Linda created and ran a homeschool program at a charter school.

During her husband's nearly 40 years of ministry, Linda has assisted in many ways. She taught Bible studies, mentored women, opened and operated a Bible college extension program, started and ran a food pantry, trained volunteers, and led worship. Linda says, "I think I am a gap-filler."

George and Linda have been married for over 38 years. They have five children whom they homeschooled for sixteen years. They also have sixteen grandchildren. They love to camp and travel. They have done short-term mission work in China, Ukraine, India, and the Philippines. George is a chaplain in the counseling department at Focus on the Family and maintains a private counseling practice.

How to contact the author:

Linda is available for speaking engagements and conferences. Contact her through the Intentional Parenting website, www.IntentionalParenting.us or at:

> Axiom Press
> 2910 N. Powers Blvd. #241
> Colorado Springs, CO   80922
> 719-299-0814
> linda@intentionalparenting.us

HERE'S WHAT PEOPLE ARE SAYING ABOUT

INTENTIONAL PARENTING:

"One of the biggest problems most of us parents have is that our kids didn't come with the instruction manual attached! Linda Stahnke has done us a wonderful favor to supply that crucial need. Written from a wealth of personal experience, she shares from her heart an abundance of practical knowledge, compassionate support, and Biblical wisdom to guide us through the complexities and challenges of parenthood. I highly recommend this fantastic and helpful book!"

>   --Rev. Jared Pingleton, Psy.D., Clinical Psychologist
>   Director of Counseling Services, Focus on the Family
>   Author of *Making Magnificent Marriages*

[Intentional Parenting is] a labor of love and the work of years of experience with God and children. It has a creative way of weaving the why's and the how's together. I love the way that it is indexed so well that a mother can just look up the section of her particular need. I love the lists of skills for various ages and was particularly thankful that Linda shared their journey with their "prodigal." I wish every young mother could have this book.

>   --Phyllis Stanley, author and teacher

"The Intentional Parenting material was a great resource for family goals, discipleship, values, and traditions. The information provided a great blueprint on how to prepare a child for their future with a strong spiritual background and faith. Linda provides practical ideas based on raising her family from home schooling to discipline to ways to make camping and holidays more memorable and how dads can be involved in parenting. My favorite section was everything a child should learn before leaving the home such as knowing how to change a tire, cook and do laundry so young adults can leave home feeling equipped to thrive in the world. I learned a lot from the material and would highly recommend it to anyone with children."

--A.R. Intentional Parenting class attendee

Table of Contents

Preface   1
    What is Intentional Parenting?

1 – Parenting Toward a Blessed Life
    or Rotten Life?   3

2 – The Case for Christian Parenting   13

3 – Parenting Pitfalls – Part 1   19
    Threatening   20
    Permissive Parent   22
    Double-Standard Parent   24
    Favoritism Parent   25
    Lazy Parent   26
    Narcissistic Parent   27
    Child-Centered Parent   28
    Unjust Parent   30

4 – Parenting Pitfalls – Part 2   32
    Harsh Parent   32
    Unprotective Parent   35
    Rule-Driven Parent   36
    Indecisive Parent   38
    Buddy Parent   40
    Reactionary Parent   41
    It's All Good Parent   42
    Enabling Parent   43
    The Goal   45

5 – The Abusive Parent   46

6 – Make Yours a House of Love   52

7 – Importance of Marriage and the Home	60
Special Situations – Single Parents, Deployed Parents, Living with Grandparents, etc, 73	
8 – The Anger Remedy	81
9 – Starting with Family Goals	89
10 – The Uniqueness of Each Child	98
Gifted Children 100	
Learning Styles 102	
11 – Character Training	106
12 – Teaching Respect	115
How to Raise a Narcissist 120	
What not to Respect 129	
13 – Requiring Obedience	133
Control v. Training Chart 135	
14 – The Correction Process	142
15 – Understanding Rebellion	158
If YOU were a Rebel 160	
Identifying Rebellion 161	
Strong-Willed Child 163	
Teen Rebellion 164	
PKs & MKs 165	
16 – Specific Behavior Problems A to Z – GIANT CHAPTER!	167

17 – What Do Children Need to Learn?		225
Toddlers	227	
Ages 3-5	227	
Ages 5-7	228	
Ages 8-10	229	
Ages 10-14	230	
Ages 15-18	231	
High School-Adult	235	
Cooking Skills	241	
18 – Spiritual Life		245
19 – Making the Teen Years Great		264
Dating or Courtship?	273	
How to be a Better Listener	283	
Fad or Danger	286	
Youth Groups	292	
Teen Rebellion	293	
Teen Suicide	294	
Career Choices	295	
Preparation for Marriage	298	
20 – Adult Children & Prodigals		305
Appendix 1 – How to Choose a Church		319
Appendix 2 – ABC List of Scriptures to Memorize		320
Appendix 3 – Clothing List		323
Index		

Preface
What is Intentional Parenting?

A couple of years ago a young woman came to me, asking me to become her mentor for parenting and for being a wife. She had grown up in a dysfunctional family with parents she described as "hippies". There had often been no money for rent, but somehow there was money for drugs. There was a dislike of all kinds of authority. She finished high school while living in a foster home. She was the only one of the siblings in that family who had not gone to jail. She loved the Lord, she and her husband served the Lord, but she didn't know what to do to be a good wife and mother. She had been watching our family, and liked what she saw.

    I agreed to become her mentor, and over the course of the next year or so, she and I talked about everything in this book. We went on to teach it as a Sunday school class at our church. As a wife of 37 plus years, mother of 5 successful adult children, and a grandmother of 16 glorious grandchildren, I knew what worked for us, and what hadn't. My husband and I had been intentional and Biblical in our parenting as much as we knew how. My young friend and her husband brought their fresh experience and stories to our class as they parented three young children. It was but a few steps farther to turn our class into a book.

Perhaps you are from a dysfunctional family background and want help to make sure your children turn out well. Perhaps you are ready to embrace the hard work of parenting, but don't know where to start. This book is for you.

I encourage you to discuss each chapter with your spouse and talk about actual steps you can take in your home to institute what you are learning. If you are a wife reading this book, draw your husband in. It works better to be on the same page while you are parenting. If you are parents of teens and want to skip ahead to the chapter on the teen years, by all means, do so. Just be sure to come back to the other chapters and check to make sure you have the foundational pieces in your parenting plan as well.

Intentional Parenting is all about choosing your path, planning what to train into your children and how to go about it. It is the opposite of simply reacting to whatever comes up. It is the opposite of going with the cultural flow that surrounds your family. It is choosing to set yourself and your child(ren) up for success as adults and as believers in Christ.

Chapter 1

Parenting Toward a Blessed Life or Rotten Life?

Choose Life

Even though God had already brought the nation of Israel out of Egyptian slavery, God offered them the choice between living life as his people or of living life their own way. God confronted the entire nation with the choice. He described in detail what each lifestyle would look like. If they chose to belong to Him and to obey Him, they would have a full and rich life. They would be blessed in the city and in the field. They would be blessed in their storage and savings. If they were disobedient and lived in opposition to His ways, they would reap misery, including defeat at the hands of their enemies, crop failure, and starvation. They would even come to the desperate point of cannibalism. What a stark picture! (Read Deuteronomy chapters 6 and 28.) Today we can choose to obey the Lord, to follow His principles and thus live a blessed life. I believe that is especially true with parenting.

I find it most interesting that God dealt with the nation of Israel as families and as groups of families or tribes. Today each family has the same opportunity to choose either a blessed life or a difficult life by choosing to do things God's way. Parents are in charge of the choices for their family. When your children become adults, they will get to choose for their families.

God's mandate to parents, and incidentally to grandparents, was that they teach their children and their grandchildren. They were to speak of what they had seen, to talk to their children about what their experiences were with God, of what they had seen God do. They were to talk about it (in today's terms) when they were sitting at the dinner table and when they were driving down the road, when they were at the mall and when they were in the doctor's office.

How contrary that is to one line of modern thinking that parents should not impose their values on their children. These misguided experts mistakenly think kids can choose for themselves when they get older without ever having had any guidance from parents. What foolishness. God meant for each successive generation to train the next generation through their experiences and knowledge. How else can one create a legacy?

Obviously a lack of training in other kinds of knowledge (such as technology or medicine) doesn't work that way. If we had to start over in each generation rather than to build upon prior knowledge in any given industry, we would be constantly re-learning the most basic things. It is even more important in spiritual things. Our children can stand on our shoulders having learned all we can impart to them, and live an even stronger Christian life than we have. My husband and I marvel that our grown children are better parents than we were at their age; that they have so much more on track in their lives than we did.

Imagine your children understanding their destiny at a younger age than you did. Imagine them having fewer struggles with obedience to God. Imagine them fulfilling their life purpose sooner, affecting change in society, and living out godly character better than you did. Imagine them running, not walking, in service to their fellow man for the sake of the gospel. My heart cries, "May it be so!" But this cannot happen if you withhold your knowledge from your children.

Option 1

Besides saying parents should not impose their values on their children, there are some other worldly ideas that keep creating dysfunctional young people. One problem is that parents are too busy with their careers and their own self-fulfillment to take time to parent. Children are left to raise themselves and to figure out life on their own, even though they may have a roof over their heads and food on the table. These parents may say they give their children quality time, if not quantity time. (Children need BOTH!) Worse yet, they may give money or large gifts instead of giving them time at all, trying to soothe the parent's guilty conscience.

Another problem is that some parents are unrealistic. They are surprised by misbehavior. Perhaps they do not believe in the existence of the sin nature. Maybe they thought that parenting would be all sweetness and light, fun and games. Real life comes as a shock to them when their 2-year old stamps his foot and yells, "No!" They are surprised by willful disobedience. They were sure their child would be their friend! They hoped to parent as a buddy. (More on this in later chapters.) Not so!

Another common mindset is accepting or tolerating misbehavior. They think that bad behavior is a phase, and that it will go away after a time, that the child will outgrow the problem. People may say, "Boys will be boys." They may accept misbehavior as normal.

Some parents hope for the best without training for the best. They may tend to discipline their children only

Intentional Parenting

when they are embarrassed or personally offended by some remark or action. They may be the kind of parent who ignores misbehavior again and again, only to blow up when as an adult they can't take anymore.

Look around you. There are plenty of examples of how this is working out for our society. Adults and children both think the world surely should revolve around them. Basic civility and manners are rarely seen. Many people, old and young, are prone to outburst of anger, rage and violence. Increasingly, teen suicide is shocking and grieving us all.

It's a Battle Out There

Parenting is a hard job. But there are some forces at work in our culture that make it even harder. One is the media. You know – TV comedies, movies, and pop culture books. Parents are depicted as stupid or at least out of touch with kids and modern times. TV parents are easy to deceive. TV kids know best. Some show seem to depict the teenagers as living independently of any adults.

And then there's school. Our educational system is by definition focused on a humanistic world view. They teach that mankind can save himself. They seek to impose their values on society and indoctrinate our children in secularism. Parents who want to know what is going on with their child and insist on maintaining their values may be considered problematic to school staff, perhaps even intolerant and even dangerous.

So called experts on child-rearing appear everywhere like so many talking heads. People who have rejected scriptural principles look for answers on how to fix their families, looking anywhere other than the Bible or church in order to find help or affirmation. Some experts are very permissive in their philosophy, teaching that the parent should follow the child's lead, that the child's feelings and happiness take priority over what is right or wrong. Others present partial truths, watered down without the strong mandate for obeying God or dealing with sinfulness.

We cannot parent like secular people and expect to raise Christ-like children. Scripture says we have three enemies: the world, the flesh and the devil. The world wants to make us like them. They want us to go with the flow, to fit in with them and not make anyone uncomfortable. The Bible says if we love the world (and its ways), the love of the Father is not in us.

Then there is our own flesh, meaning our carnal selves. This can be our worst enemy. Our desires battle within us: selfishness, greed, fears, and so on. Pride, laziness and rebellion wait for us in weak moments. Sometimes our flesh rules our choices, our values and our parenting.

Lastly, there's Satan, our arch enemy. He promotes distance from God or rebellion against Him. Satan encourages exaltation of our own ideas, especially if they disagree with scripture. He elevates things that are occultic or demonic, often coating them with a veneer of mystery or making darkness tantalizing.

Option 2 – Intentional Parenting

The truth is that parents have good days and bad days. We know our children and the tricks they try to pull. We know what is good, what is right and wrong and what we want for them. Sometimes we have a vague sense that something is not right, but we are not sure what to do about it.

And we know that discipline issues often arise at the moments when we least feel capable of dealing with them. We may be tired or busy or distracted. We may have just gotten comfortable on the couch. Perhaps our movie is just at the good part, or the food we are cooking might burn. Murphy's Law is very real to parents. Not only do bad or difficult things with our kids come up, but often at the worst possible moments.

We *always* have a choice. And not to train IS to train. If we allow kids to continue in what is wrong, we are building into them that practice. **Let me repeat: what we ALLOW is being trained into our children.** If we default to what is easy in parenting, we will reap what the average parent in our society is reaping these days.

The Bible confronts us with a tough question: Do you love your child or do you hate them? Proverbs 13:24 and Hebrews 12:6-8 say that if you do not discipline your child, you prove that you *hate* them. Strong words, but they are God's! Lazy parenting is something far worse that we originally thought.

Once, when I was feeling the weight of parenting and homeschooling our five kids ages seven to thirteen, I stepped out of my back door to get a breath of air and tried to re-group my thoughts. There was my neighbor lady, lying in the sun in her bikini (of course, looking fit and skinny!). I said, "Aw, Lord, it's just not fair! Why do I have to work so HARD?!" That still small voice said, "I require more of you." How could I argue with that?

Intentional Parenting

Good parenting is sacrificial. It costs time, energy and money. It requires that you be an example, not just a talking head. It means that you must often do things you do not want to do, like confronting bad behavior or spanking. It often means giving up doing what you want to do when you want to do it. And it means you keep on doing that again and again. There is no substitute for consistency.

But here's the kicker: **YOU CAN PUT YOURSELF IN A POSITION TO SUCCEED.** The choices you make about how you are going to parent will drive how you live life during middle age and beyond. You can choose the harder road on the front end, but the bigger blessings later on. You can set a course, do the work, make a plan, and prioritize what's right. You will be choosing to reap the benefits, to bask in the joys, to revel in the fun of well-behaved children who become accomplished adults. Pr. 29:17 says, (my paraphrase) "Discipline your son while there is time and he will give you rest."

Many parents who have battled and battled strong-willed children will tell you that the breakthrough came eventually. The joy a parent experiences when they see their child fulfilling their destiny is built on the back of hard work in the younger years. Good parenting is more than just getting kids to obey. It is teaching them to think, giving them the tools to be internally motivated to make right choices.

In some ways, parenting is like giving birth. Once you are in the middle of it, you can't call a halt and give up. It usually turns out that labor is so much tougher than a mom ever imagined. But you'll find the woman who has been though labor and delivery has a new kind of strength. She has accomplished something amazing and wonderful. Shortly after the pain and difficulty, she is basking in the joy of holding that newborn.

So make the decision. Embrace the hard work. Choose the blessed life. It's time to move forward and create a plan for success through intentional parenting.

Endnotes

Blessing or cursed? Deuteronomy 6:1-11, Deuteronomy 28
Three enemies: 1 John 2:15-16
Carnal / fleshly nature: Galatians 5:19-21
Comparing wisdom: James 3:13-18
Sin nature: Romans 1:18, 5:12, 3:23, 6:23 and Ephesians 2:8, 9

Chapter 2
The Case for Christian Parenting

Authority

I believe that the Bible is the true word of God. It expresses His heart and His instructions for living in this world. It teaches us how to prepare for the next world. The Bible forms the foundation for my authority as a parent. Because God made all creatures, He has ownership of them. His design is unique. He made me the way I am to fit the destiny He has in mind for me and for the part I am to play in His kingdom. That makes me valuable to God. It makes others valuable as well. (Our founding fathers noted this in our Declaration of Independence: we are endowed *by our creator* with certain inalienable rights… all men are created equal…)

This view is basic to our identity. It is also basic to our value system. The respect for God's ownership of all creation is part of what is called "The Fear of the Lord." God is a big god. His understanding is perfect. He is the boss. I must obey Him or there will be consequences. God has delegated some of His authority to parents. We are given a solemn charge to raise our children in a way that leads them to a blessed life. And just as we want to please our Creator-

God, our children should have a healthy fear of displeasing us. They should know that there are consequences waiting in the wings for bad behavior.

Correction and affirmation are two sides of the same coin. In a two-parent home, neither parent should always be the heavy-handed one or always the pleasant and approving one. Sometimes you see one parent functioning as the toughie, and the other compensating by being a full of mercy and grace, perhaps even a push-over. Both parents need to balance themselves out and exemplify to their children a blend of a caring and, when necessary, correcting presence. In this way, we are portraying the balance that exists in who God is. It is better for a child to see two balanced parents, wise and discerning, than for them to see parenting as a tug-of-war between competing philosophies. Discuss things with your spouse and become united in how you handle matters. George and I frequently said to our children, "Mommy and Daddy always agree!" Of course, there were times when we didn't actually agree, so we excused ourselves to another room to have a private discussion. (PLEASE, do not argue in front of the children!) When we came out of that room we had agreed on a united approach for dealing with the question or misbehavior at hand. (Single parents, do not be discouraged. I'll address your special concerns in chapter 7.)

A Solemn Duty

It is God who charges parents with raising their children in the nurture and admonition of the Lord. This means we are to teach and model for our children what He is like, what pleases Him, how to live according to the Bible. God commands parents to do this, and promises blessing if we are obedient. We have both the authority and the responsibility to parent. Who you are and what you do are important to your child's well-being and identity. How you parent is important to God.

He also commands that children are to obey parents. The first commandment with a promise attached is that children honor their fathers and mothers, and they will then receive long life. My grandmother and her mother (both of whom died into their mid-90s) said that scripture had been the reason for their longevity.

It is a given that the child's will and the parents' will clash from time to time. Scripture says that foolishness is bound up in the heart of a child. It may be demonstrated by childish lack of perspective or by willful disobedience and temper tantrums. It is the parent's job to train foolishness out and wisdom into a child. No matter how intelligent your child may be, you still have work to do. You must train them.

When our children misbehave, it reflects on us. We are called to correct that foolishness, so that our children will not be set up for a messed up life or an early death. (More on correction methods in chapter 14.)

As children of God, we are to please the Lord. That is a good model for our children. They should want to please us. We can tell our children, when they do what is right, they will be happy. We will be happy. When they do what wrong, it makes us all sad. (*Never* say that we cease to love them. Love is not based on performance.) Life is just better for everyone when they choose good things.

Not parenting out of fear

Many parents say to themselves, "I don't want to be like *my* parents. I'm not going to do things the way they did." They choose which kinds of correction they will use or perhaps not to correct at all based on the pain of how their parents did or did not work with them. If your parents were either physically or verbally abusive, those memories may haunt your parenting. You may be afraid of being like your parents.

Intentional parenting requires thinking through responses and planning ahead for how to handle situations. It is one of the tools you can use to prevent many parenting mistakes. You have the opportunity to **SET YOURSELF UP FOR SUCCESS**. By setting goals and planning how you will discipline ahead of time, you can avoid some of the pitfalls that come during emotional high-pressure moments. Be sure to ask the Lord for His help. Pray, ask Him to remind you in the moment when you might overreact or say the wrong thing. Take a few extra seconds before responding to your children, especially when you are angry. Don't lash out with your first reaction when things are crazy.

You may be afraid of making mistakes with your children. Frankly, it is likely that you will make a mistake at some point or another. If that happens, you must apologize to your child, start over, and do the right thing from then on. Don't expect them to buy your act if you just try to bluff your way through.

Coming to Faith Later in Parenting
If you came to faith later in life, perhaps when your children were already teenagers, you need to lay some ground work. Explain to your children how your life and your thinking has

been changed. Talk to them about your new faith, about your desire to please God, about how the Bible will guide your thinking and decision making from now on. You may need to apologize for your past mistakes or bad example. Be sure to give them time to assimilate this new way of life. Don't be afraid to raise the bar on your family standards. Just discuss it ahead of time. If they struggle with all this, be patient. Keep loving. Continue to model the changes. Explain the moral and Biblical reasons for your decisions and new values.

If you are the first in your family to become a Christian, embrace the fact that change starts with you. You are beginning a new way of life, a blessed life. You are starting a *new* legacy.

Endnotes

Authority of the Bible: 2 Timothy 4:16-17
Nurture and Admonition of the Lord: Eph. 6:4;
Train a child: Proverbs 22:6
Command to parents and grandparents: Deuteronomy 4:9-10; Psalm 78:4-7
Children to be obedient: Exodus 20:12, Ephesians 6:1-2
Foolishness: Proverbs 22:15
Saved from early death: Proverbs 23:13-14
Desiring to please the Lord: 2 Corinthians 5:9
The Fear of the Lord by John Bevere is an excellent study on this subject. I recommend both the book and the DVD series. His definition of the fear of the Lord is wonderfully balanced without just calling it "respect". He also weaves in the awe that should be present.

Chapter 3
Parenting Pitfalls – Part 1

Maybe you don't know very many successful parents. Maybe your parents didn't do a very good job and you know more things from them that you *don't* want to do than things *to* do. Maybe you find yourself being like your parent in ways that aren't good or positive. How can you change? How can you be different?

Your Parenting Wardrobe

There's a great pattern in Ephesians 4:28 and Colossians 3:8 and 12 that you can apply to your ways as a parent, and later in how to train your child. It's a bit like getting dressed. You put off the old ways and put on some new ones. You stop doing the things that are ineffective or negative, and start doing things that are productive and Biblical.

The Ephesians scripture about stealing says the thief must do three things: he must 1) Stop stealing, and 2) Work to provide for his own needs. Beyond the obvious actions, the heart must change. Rather than being a taker, he must become a giver. Step 3 is to give to the poor. This shows he has truly put off and put on new behavior.

Intentional Parenting

Here are some examples of poor parenting practices and their opposites that should replace them.

The Threatening Parent

Can your child count to 3 (or 5, or 10) because you're always counting before making them obey you? Have you trained them not to obey until after a countdown? Do you repeat your commands over and over, only to have children ignore until you raise your voice or get up off the couch to come after them? Obedience isn't about your ego, or your peace. It is for the sake of the child. While you may think counting to give your child the opportunity to obey is being gracious and merciful, you are actually teaching them not to obey you.

First-time obedience, even immediate obedience, may be the difference between a serious injury and safety. We began working with our children at about 6 months of age to teach them the meaning of the word, "No." At this young age, we had only one or two things that were no-no's. It might be touching electronic equipment or knick-knacks. These things were training grounds, opportunities for the child to learn that we would be firm about "No," and that there were consequences (a slap of the hand, perhaps) for disobeying. We would move the child away from the object and wait to make sure they did not go back to it. As they got older, we required them to obey quickly and without arguing, whining or crying. We said, "Obey quickly and quietly." Our daughter, Melody, has added "and fully" for her children.

Amanda was our child who ran everywhere rather than walking. She was very high energy. At about 3 she was running between cars, headed into the path of an oncoming car she could not see. From some distance away I yelled, "Amanda, STOP!!" She screeched to a halt, leaning backwards dramatically. The car went "whiff" right in front of her, inches away. Thank God she obeyed instantly!! We both cried and I praised her quick obedience.

So if you put off threatening, what do you put on? You must mean what you say, say what you mean. You must be ready to follow through to make obedience mandatory. First ask yourself, do I mean what I am saying? Is this the time to do this, or am I really giving them a warning that the time is approaching for dinner? If it's not really time to come to the table, but you want them to obey in 10 minutes, why not say, "Dinner will be ready in 10 minutes. Wind up what you are doing and then go wash your hands." Set yourself and your child up for success, rather than setting up a time of wrangling over washing their hands for the next 10 minutes.

If you are considering an activity or want to verbally process with your child about something, make it clear that this is a discussion. When your decision is made, follow through. An example might be choosing a movie. This could involve a discussion about choices open to the child. You limit it to two or three you are willing to consider. They may offer a fourth option. If this is a discussion, not an argument, that's fine. When you finalize a decision, be firm. The discussion is over. They cannot continue to argue about your choice and you threaten to have no movie. They can watch with everyone else, or go play in their room. End of story.

Jesus said, Let your yes be yes and your no be no. Anything more is a trap. Set yourself up for success.

The Permissive Parent

Some parents hate to ever tell their child no. Here are some possible reasons for this:

- Weak standards – They don't have strong beliefs themselves about right and wrong. Perhaps they accept worldliness or cultural priorities (beauty, youth, etc.) rather than moral mandates. For example, it's okay to go to popular movies or watch trashy sitcoms.

Never mind discretion in our choices. Everyone else is watching it, so it must be okay, right?

- More concerned about their child's feelings than the truth. They might rather clean coloring off the wall that tell their child they cannot do that.
- Lazy – don't want to take time or energy to correct. Don't want to face the battle.
- Think the child is SO smart they don't need correction.
- Are embarrassed about their own guilt and failures. For example, how can you tell your child not to use vulgar language if they hear you doing so yourself.
- Trying to compensate for other areas – divorce, loss of finances, etc.

A permissive parent may try to hover over their child and block them from getting in trouble or getting hurt. This is not a good idea. You will not be able to be there for every event or opportunity. Teach them to make wise choices even when you are not around.

Put on:

- Awareness of the sin nature

- Embrace the job of parenting – be willing to do the work necessary to lead to a blessed life.
- Give your children values
- Correct as needed. Think about what this behavior looks like in 5 years... As an adult? Their boss will not be sweet and permissive. They will yell at them and fire them. Teach them what is right and good. Draw standards and principles from scripture.

The Double-Standard Parent

"Do as I say, not as I do." Need I say more? This statement gets groans from those who have attended my parenting classes. I think it is one of the most despised things young parents identify; it is the thing that they universally hated in how they were parented. Hypocrisy in the home is one of the main reasons young people raised in church do not continue in church after leaving home.

The best way to be a model your children can emulate is to be a principle-centered person. Base your life and decisions on principles that are timeless, not circumstances that change. Talk with them about choices and the moral reasons why you do what you do. Build into them a filing system of ideas and concepts that they can draw from when they face life's difficulties.

The Favoritism Parent

Throughout the stories of Isaac, Jacob and Joseph, we see the devastating effects of favoritism on families. It breeds hatred between siblings. Kids will play tricks on each other, trying to get more attention or favor. Kids will say mean things to each other if they feel less love or approval, trying to raise themselves in the pecking order. While some of our children may be easier to raise and some may have qualities that are harder to live with, we must make every effort to treat our children the same. Rules for behavior must be consistent. Gift-giving needs to be equal (in number and in value) as much as is possible. Quality time must be measured out to all. Clothing provision must be approximately the same.

I used to apologize to my children if I found something for one and not the others at a garage sale. I would try to make sure they had about the same number of clothing items (pants, shirts, sox, etc.). Do not give the enemy a foothold to lie to your children about your love.

Be careful of always correcting the obviously difficult child and not noticing the more discreet child who is also misbehaving. You can find yourself disciplining that difficult child so often that you mistakenly think the others are doing fine. One or more of the others may be just under your radar. Give all your children the benefit of being trained to your family standard.

The Lazy Parent

Murphy's Law of Parenting should probably read, "Whenever your children are going to get into trouble, it will probably be at the worst possible moment and when you are the most tired." Parenting is hard work. You may have to stop what you are doing to go address behavior. Just when you get comfortable on the couch, you'll hear, "Mommy, I need to go potty." You will have to get up in the night to take care of a sick child and clean up smelly messes. About the time you're having an important conversation on the phone the kids will knock over the lamp while chasing the dog through the house. You get the idea. Parenting is inconvenient and tiring. You work, discipline kids, and clean things up. Then you do it again.

But the truer picture is that parenting is an investment. You do a lot of work on the front end, but on the back end you enjoy your children. And, not surprisingly, the opposite is true. If you are unwilling to put in the work that training children requires, you will find yourself working harder with them, maybe even going to court and paying lawyers to help with the messes they make later in life.

The Narcissistic Parent
Our society is filled with people who are completely self-centered. Ez. 16:4-5 talks about unnatural parents who are able to forget their children. It may be manifested by a life focused on personal interests rather than the family, or priorities like going to the gym, being with friends, and taking time for oneself instead of caring for children. Children may be just an add-on or an inconvenience. Some parents are so tied up with their work that they do not have time to listen to their children or go to their school to straighten out problems. It breaks my heart to hear about how children need to take care of themselves and look out for themselves and fight for themselves. Parents should be their children's biggest fans and best advocates. If a child is not turning in homework or is being bullied at school, Dad, Mom, take off work, haul yourself down there and meet with that teacher or that principal! For Pete's sake, don't wait until your child gets hurt, turns to others for help, or even commits suicide in

Intentional Parenting

desperate hopelessness. (This happened with a high school student in our city last year.) Some of the nonsense I read about teaching children to be independent is a smoke screen for parents who are too busy to show up and parent. The Family Medical Leave Act (FMLA) provides for you to take off work (without pay) to take care of urgent family business. Sometimes being a parent is sacrificial. Just do it.

The Child-Centered Parent

By far, this is the most common thing I see in struggling parents. By focusing on the child, rather than on the family, parents may allow the child to be in charge. She becomes the little tyrant of the house. She is demanding and even rude. Life revolves around her likes and dislikes. Mom fixes her a different meal. Her tantrums control where, when, and if the family can go anywhere. Sometimes these parents are just waiting for the child to go to school in order for someone else to make them behave. You are not doing them any favors by allowing them to wait until then. Make your child mind you. Teach your child to consider others. Make the good of the entire family a priority. If your children are older, take them to work at a soup kitchen or food pantry to learn to appreciate what they have and see how others who

Intentional Parenting

are less fortunate live. Discuss those who've been through natural disasters like Hurricane Sandy and do a family project to raise money to donate to the Salvation Army or other effective charities.

One simple project to improve your child's behavior and to put off child-centeredness is by not allowing them to interrupt you when you are talking to other adults. Rather than allow them to interrupt at will, have them put their hand on your arm or leg to let you know they are waiting to talk to you. Be brief in wrapping up your point with your adult friend and then turn to your child to see what they need. Teach them to control themselves and put concerns of others ahead of their own. (Emergencies excepted, of course.)

Teach children to be considerate of other family members. Discuss how their behavior affects others in the household. Talk about how their words make the other person feel. We used an egg timer for kids who interrupted siblings, demanding attention immediately. The offender could not speak for 3 minutes while the salt trickled down in the glass. That helped them learn to wait their turn.

Teach children to be considerate of older people or of handicapped people in the store and at church. Children who are allowed to run through the foyer at church could knock

Intentional Parenting

an elderly person down. Have them let a wheelchair-bound person go first while they hold the door.

Set some boundaries. Teach your child that there are appropriate places to play, and some that are off-limits. Tell your child they cannot play or explore the platform at church. There is expensive equipment up there that is not for children to touch. Libraries are quiet; wedding receptions are about the bride and groom – these are not places to run around or play. This isn't about raining on your child's parade, but teaching them appropriate behavior they will always find useful. By being the pro-active guide of your child's behavior you can set then up for success in any environment.

The Unjust Parent

There are always at least two sides to every story. And of course, it's usually the second (or third) offender who gets caught. Before you wade into a discipline problem or lash out in anger at misbehavior, take time to get all the facts. You will save having to apologize to your children for blowing it. (Yup, I said apologize.) The Bible says, "He who states his case first sees right, until his rival comes and cross-examines him." By taking time to clarify your information, you can deal with situations judiciously and avoid being an unjust parent.

You may feel challenged by these negative ideas. Some you have seen, some you may have done yourself. Let this be a turning point for you. Identify your area of need. Reverse course. Make the changes. Be the parent you were meant to be.

Endnotes

Matthew 5:37
James 1:19
Prov. 18:17
Sin nature: Romans 1:18, 5:12, 3:23, 6:23 and Ephesians 2:8, 9

Chapter 4
Parenting Pitfalls – Part 2

If you didn't find yourself in the last chapter, perhaps you might fit into one of the following additional categories.

The Harsh Parent

Sometimes, in desperation, parents speak or yell harshly at their children. They may say they are, "trying to get through to them." Or they may just be frustrated at having to deal with the same behavior again and again. Some parents are demeaning. Some are perfectionistic with nothing ever being good enough.

Scripture says, "Man's anger does not promote the righteousness God wishes and requires." You will not get what you want by being harsh. Instead it crushes the spirit of the child. It wounds inwardly. And I can promise you Satan will replay it through your child's head again and again. He will use it to breed hurt, resentment and eventually bitterness.

Educators are taught that children need seven affirmations for each correction. With the amount of correction some toddlers require, I'm not sure that is even possible. But at least I would try to balance it out. If you are the parent who does most of the correcting, make sure that you make times to hold your child and affirm them. Work at "catching" them doing something right and praise them for it. Don't fall into the trap of always being harsh and disapproving. **Practice being firm and gentle rather than firm and harsh.**

Anger can also sneak up on you, leading to physical and verbal abuse when you would rationally never consider doing such a thing. Don't even *start* to go there. Don't set yourself up by saying things like, "If you do ____, I will be SO angry!" Plan ahead for success by saying, "If you do ____, I will have to have you stand in the corner for 15 minutes." Prepare yourself to react rationally, even dispassionately. Calmly explain to your child how their behavior has hurt you or others. Remind them of what is expected through past training. Don't yell or talk down to them.

If you find your emotions soaring in the heat of the moment, give *yourself* a time-out. Tell the child they need to lay on their beds until you cool down and can deal with them. (Let them sweat the consequences for a while.) Take time to pray or stomp around your room. Talk to yourself. Cool off. Then deal with things calmly.

Intentional Parenting

I had the opportunity to learn to do this when my children were small. One day when I was expecting some ladies to come over and do some home canning, I was stressed and getting the house cleaned up and ready. The kids knew I was distracted and took advantage of it. They went into the bathroom, turned on the water and set the plug in the sink. Then they came out and locked the door behind them. Much later I discovered several inches of water in the hallway and the locked door. I could hear the water still running. I made a mad dash for a screwdriver in the junk drawer so I could get in and shut off the water, yelling at the kids all the while. After I turned off the water, I told them I was too angry to discipline them. I knew I would hurt them. And I was honest enough to realize that my stress was making everything worse. They would have to lie on their beds until I calmed down. I went on to clean up the mess, then I heard the water running in the other bathroom. Yup. The other bathroom. Thankfully, they'd not gotten the plug set well in that one. But that crazy experience was a "win" for me because I dealt with it successfully, not in my anger.

Intentional Parenting

The Unprotective Parent

Some parents are so concerned about what others think about them or about displeasing family members that they let go of protecting their child. There are times when parents have to make inconvenient or awkward choices in order to protect their children. It may be something as small as saying no to a movie others think is fine, or it may be a serious as skipping a family gathering where inappropriate behavior is accepted.

You may have a family member who is not safe for your children to be around. You know that they may mistreat your child or provide them with alcohol at a young age. Perhaps they are prone to talking negatively about you or disagreeing with your values in front of the child.

These folks may whine and ask why you won't let them baby-sit. They may say you are not a good Christian, and that you are unforgiving. They may try to manipulate you into doing what they want. You may have tried and tried to work with them in the past, only to get burned.

DON'T DO IT!! It is your job to protect your child and to hold firm about your family standards. You may spare them from something that could affect them for years. Your firm choice may prevent months or years of therapy.

Intentional Parenting

There are options. You may need to limit your children's time with some family members or only allow visits when you can be present at all times. You may have to leave a function early if activities that run counter to your values arise. So be it! Your child is more valuable than someone else's feelings.

The Rule-Driven Parent
Sometimes it seems easy to make a rule for each misbehavior that comes up. They misbehave. You make a rule against it. You might say, "There. That eliminates that behavior." That sort of legalism does not work in a lasting way with children. In fact, children who are raised with lots of restrictions without the reasoning to back them up tend to eventually rebel or throw off restraint. When they become adults, they run the other way – often with a vengeance!

Try broad rules that cover a number of issues. One example would be, "We treat others the way we would like to be treated." That covers name-calling, meanness, lying, and so on. The reason for the rule would be because they, too, are God's creation and valued by Him. Another example might be, "If you take out the toys, you have to clean them up."

If you are prone to saying, "Do it because I said so!" how will your child behave when you are not there? What they really need are the answers to those incessant "Why" questions. Practice being a principle-centered parent. By explaining the moral reason why they can or cannot do something, you are creating a filing system in their heads. They can later draw on this information for making solid, wise decisions about potential choices when you are not there to make a rule. When they are old enough, show them the scripture verses by which you make your decisions. Here is where the Bible has more authority than you do.

I grew up in a family with certain rules about dress. They were beliefs my parents had been taught, but I could not find them in scripture. They were preferences, not principles from the Bible. For example, I was not allowed to wear pants. Instead, I taught my children the principles of modesty in dress, a lasting principle.

There is an exception to explaining everything. I'm not suggesting you try to reason with a 2 or 3-year old. Small children need to obey first, and then after obeying receive explanations or teaching on why you required what you did. For older children the explanation can be a part of the command. For example, "You may not play in the front yard without a grownup present. I feel that you are safer playing in the backyard where there is a fence." Another example is, "Do not lie. People will not believe what you say if you are known to lie. And God says lying is a sin." (Rev. 21:8) Or, "Do not hit your brother. It hurts him physically and it hurts his feelings that you would do that. You two want to be friends all your lives, so do things that help your friendship to grow, not ruin it."

Let your training toward moral thinking and decision-making fill your child with wisdom for the future. They can throw off your rules, but they can't get away from what is right and wrong.

The Indecisive Parent

Some parents have trouble with being firm when making decisions. They may delay and delay in making a decision, or they may make a decision then pull it back and change their mind. Maybe they say a child cannot have a snack then a few minutes later give them one. Or the parent may say the child cannot have dessert unless they finish all their food, then change their mind when everyone else has dessert. This sends a message that your word means nothing. A child only has to wait or whine or throw a fit to get what they want eventually.

Perhaps this parent wants to be gracious or maybe they are afraid of making a wrong move. Perhaps they are plagued by self-doubt. The Bible speaks of this wavering when you need wisdom as being "double-minded" and says don't think you'll get anything from God if you are this way. Yikes! That's pretty strong.

Unfortunately, this is also like blood in the water to a strong-willed child. They will play you, argue with your decisions, work you to get their way eventually, knowing they can wear you down. And if you let your child bully you (yes, bully!) you will find yourself becoming resentful toward them. It will color our responses to them. And do you think they will not notice it? Children sense what is going on with us.

This is a downward spiral. Stop right now. Put off this kind of parenting. Be a strong parent. Don't be afraid of being the parent. You probably will make some mistakes. God knew that when he gave you that child. Your child may not like you when you have to be tough with him. That's okay. You'll be friends after they grow up. Choose to be strong. Be the parent. If you delay, the work needed to turn this child around will multiply.

One of the blessings of firmness is that it creates a sense of security in your child. They know where the boundaries are and that they will be there each time. Of course, they will test the boundaries from time to time, checking to see if they can cross the line, but a little firmness will let them know they are still there and the child will be happy. If you find you have made a mistake with a decision, apologize and do better next time.

Dads, back your wives up and put the kibosh on letting your kids run her ragged. Do not allow ongoing arguing over something that has been settled.

Do you think God is ever indecisive? I don't think so. There is no weakness in him. One Old Testament law ordered that a continually rebellious son was to be put to death (probably referred to a teenager or young man). This is illegal in our society, but it shows you how serious this is to God. Be firm and decisive.

The Buddy Parent

Some parents aren't parents. They try to be their child's buddy. They want to do fun things together and not have to correct their child. They want the child to behave like a friend would. They want to be liked by their child.

Intentional Parenting

This robs the child of having a parent, of having someone who will teach them about life and correct them when they go the wrong direction. They will be less secure, less confident, and at a loss in an adult world.

Put off being a buddy. Be the parent. That is what they need. Realize that there will be some conflicts, some negative emotions during the process of training them up to be competent young people. But if you put in the work while they are young, they will become your friends when they are adults. You will enjoy being around them. And they will have benefited from your wisdom. (More on how to deal with adult children in Chapter 20.)

The Reactionary Parent

This kind of parent only corrects or disciplines her child when she is upset. Mom may be embarrassed by the child's behavior and light into them for it. Dad may have no thought for the consistency of the behavior requirements, but just reacts in the moment.

Put on being an analytical parent. (More on how to set a family standard for behavior in Chapter 9.) Years ago when my first child was about 1 ½, he was jumping on the couch. It was a bit cute, and I was happy he was learning to jump up and down. But then that still small voice whispered, "What will this behavior look like in 5 years? Uh-oh. Not so good. Rather than allow a behavior to become entrenched that I would have to work hard to remove later, it was better not to let my son jump on the couch at all. Jumping on the floor was fine.

What about making noise in church? My angry reaction came more out of embarrassment than out of anything that would develop good behavior in church. I needed to teach my child what behavior was acceptable where, then explain to him before we went in how to behave in this venue. This would set us both up for success.

Being an analytical parent might seem like work on the front end, but you'll be much more relaxed and your children will be more peaceful knowing what to expect.

The "It's All Good" Parent

Some parents have no boundaries and do not believe in moral absolutes. Right and wrong is about what is right for you, not necessarily for everyone. Truth is truth for some, but not all.

For the Christian, this is not acceptable. God does not think that way. The Bible is full of commands and

Intentional Parenting

consequences for disobedience. Do not teach your children the false thinking of no moral absolutes. The Bible is the Word of God. God is the final authority over human behavior. God will judge sin. Explain the world as God sees it. Be firm in your beliefs and communicate them to your children.

I wish I had been firmer about the dangers of smoking and about the trap it was. Instead I didn't want to be negative about a family member who was a smoker. Later, one of my daughters took up smoking, thinking she would have some good fellowship with that family member. It took her years to get free from that.

Be honest with your child about how God sees all kinds of issues. Co-habitation (living together without marriage) is wrong. Tell them suicide is wrong. We do not have the right to decide when our lives are over. Teach them that resentment can grow to hatred and violence. They need to be quick to forgive. Don't be afraid to speak out on whatever issues arise.

The Enabling Parent

Some parents provide a safety net for their children so that they never experience consequences. Maybe they let their

Intentional Parenting

child stay home from school rather than face the music about a paper that was not finished. I watched one mother pull her toddler out of trouble over and over without ever telling him "No." The moment she was too far across the room to catch him, he burned himself on a coffee urn. Will this child grow up having no sense of boundaries? Will that child think that they are entitled to being taken care of without ever having to experience any problems?

An entitlement mentality thinks that someone owes me and that my life should be taken care of at someone else's expense. Instead of weaving that into your child's psyche, be a parent that uses natural consequences. The Bible says we reap what we sow. If a child breaks a lamp, tell them they must do chores and earn money to buy a new one. If they spend their money on something foolish, do not give them more money for something else they want.

Do not clean up your child's room when they are old enough to do so themselves. You may have to keep them from enjoying some other activity in order to get the room done. Or you may be willing to let them live in a mess (up to a point).

Do not provide all kinds of toys and unlimited media time with no corresponding requirements. Give children the opportunity to earn some things. Let some things come as a result of effort.

If they don't let you know they have an extra Scout meeting with reasonable notice (say 24 hours), you do not suddenly have an emergency to get them there.

Be careful of making up the difference in whatever happens when your child should be responsible. Allow some consequences to come home to roost and teach your child.

The Goal

Our goal is to raise children who honor God and who become more and more like Christ. That's a pretty high standard. That means that we set aside what is easy or perhaps the way we were raised, and we teach our children to obey us and God's Word. Parenting involves a lot of sowing and reaping. Be sure what you are planting with your children is what you want your crop to be.

Endnotes

Pr. 14:15-16
James 1:6-8
Deut. 21:18-21
Exodus 20 and Revelation 22:12-15
Galatians 6:7
Ephesians 2:10

Chapter 5
The Abusive Parent

Some parents have come from homes with lots of domestic violence. They may be broken adults, still in pain, unable to cope with parenting. A person who has come from this kind of background may react and become weak in parenting, over-compensating for what they went through, wanting to be the opposite of what they experienced. Or they may find themselves repeating the angry behavior or abuse they lived with. Perhaps the abusive parent feels frustrated and thinks that nothing else seems to work to get the reaction of change they want from their family members. They may not have the tools parent in any other way.

First of all, let me say that abuse is wrong. It is sinful. It is illegal. Matthew 18:6 and 10 warn that those who hurt little ones come to God's attention. Revelation states that the angry will not see heaven. These are strong words. God sees abuse as serious sin.

When I hear the stories from adults who have lived through years and years of abuse, I wonder why the other parent didn't do something to stop it. In several cases, the mother put up with the abuse of the child because she did

Intentional Parenting

not want to lose the roof over their heads. These children grow up thinking they are not worth fighting for, that they are meant for being used. They are looking at years of therapy to heal the brokenness.

If one parent is violent or abusive, the other parent should not excuse it or cover for them. If your spouse is in a rage, pack the kids up and go to a friend's house. If they won't let you leave, call 911. Tell them you will return when they are calm and ready to talk about things. Require them to go to counseling with a Biblical counselor. Tell them they must participate in doing the homework and responding to good counsel in order to keep the family united.

You must make every effort to keep the family together, if possible, while maintaining the safety of each person. It will take courage to enforce these boundaries. If you do not do this, Social Services may have to remove your children from your home. Most communities have "safe houses" for women and children who need to escape abuse and live in an unknown place.

We usually think of men as the perpetrators of domestic violence, but women can be the ones who are physically or verbally abusive as well. The same truths apply

Intentional Parenting

to keeping children safe, no matter the gender of the person with the problem.

Keeping a Clean Heart
Sometimes those who have been abused struggle with sexuality. Many women become lesbians. Some young men who've had domineering, abusive mothers become gay. Some young people fling themselves into promiscuity, looking for love and respect. If you were abused, get professional help with a good Biblical counselor. (Note: not all Christian counselors are Biblical counselors.) The sins that were committed against you do not define you. But your responses to them do. Do not make excuses for wrong responses. Choose carefully.

If abuse and rage are happening in your home, consider seeing a Biblical counselor to sort things out. *Focus on the Family* has lists of Christian counselors in most cities and even special help line for those in ministry.

Submission or Abuse?
Some Christians, and even Christian leaders, mistakenly tell women that they must put up with violence and verbal abuse. They call it submission. Domestic violence displeases God

and it is just plain illegal. 1 Peter 3 says a man who does not deal gently and kindly with his wife will find his prayers hindered.

What does real submission look like? Christian marriage is a partnership. It is working together to fulfill the purposes of God. A friend of mine has what I think is the best definition of submission. It is "aggressive support." Submission means being a super-positive cheerleader for your spouse.

So much of what women think is submission is just passivity. It is an absence of being that helper-completer. A wise woman will share her opinions (once or twice, not continually). She will bring her strengths to bear in building the family. She will use her wisdom and intuition in every positive way possible.

Many women pretend to be passive, but are full of resentment. They may try manipulation to have some sort of voice in what happens. This is not a godly way to function.

Both spouses need to bring all their strengths to the marriage to make it awesome. Rather than suppressing the skills of one partner so the other person can shine, it is best to build both up as much as possible.

Intentional Parenting

By emphasizing partnership, a couple will find themselves working together 90% of the time, or so. Then in the 5 to 10% of times when you still disagree, after discussing all the options thoroughly, after both the husband and the wife express their ideas, a decision has to be made. If they still do not agree, the woman is to yield to her husband. *This* is Biblical submission in a New Testament marriage. (If the decision turns out to be wrong, a wise woman will refrain from saying, "I told you so." We all want to be accepted and to be given room to grow, even when we make mistakes. Remember ladies, you reap what you sow.)

Modeling this kind of marriage will set the example your children will follow when they look for their spouses in the future. So what will you demonstrate? Passivity or power struggles or partnership?

Practical Matters

So what do you do on those days when you are in danger of being an abusive parent?

While spanking is a valid form of correction, swats should be limited to one or two at a time and never more than 5. Never think that you can spank a child enough times

Intentional Parenting

to change their minds or break their wills. Strong-willed or rebellious children need a longer-term process.

If you have had repeated discipline problems throughout the day and need to swat frequently, don't allow yourself to fall into the rage trap. You may need to pull the plug on everything, changing up the environment for the day. Call a halt to the merry-go-round of power struggles and create a totally different tone. Have all the kids take a nap. You might need to take a nap. Or get out of the house and go to the library or on a picnic. Call a friend for a play date. Change everything up. You are the adult. Be in charge. Make a good choice.

Endnotes

1 Corinthians 5:17
Focus on the Family. 1-800-A FAMILY and Parsonage.org. They keep a list of Christian counselors across the country.
Renewal Ministries of Colorado Springs www.renewalcs.org

Chapter 6
Make Yours a House of Love

Living a Life of Love

Throughout the New Testament we are commanded to live and exemplify the love God has for us. Ephesians 5:2 says we are to live a life of love. And Jesus said it was one way people would know we were His disciples. Sometimes it is easier to love other believers than it is to love our own family. Walking in love daily requires living with others' idiosyncrasies and inadequacies. In parenting, we must love enough to discipline our children. It is for their own good.

In addition to healthy training and discipline, what are some other ways we can live a life of love in our homes?

- Love your spouse. Let the children see that you admire and care for each other. Speak positively about your spouse. Take care of disagreements in private. Seeing parents fight makes children insecure. They wonder if the parents are going to split up, divorce, or if one parent will be leaving. Sure grown-ups have conflicts. Just don't do so in front of the children.

Intentional Parenting

- Root for the success of each family member. Be happy for one another when someone achieves a goal or overcomes an obstacle. Don't let jealousy prevent sincere congratulations. Celebrate together when someone has a victory.
- It almost goes without saying that not allowing name-calling, cut-downs and sarcasm is primo to having a house of love. This seems popular in TV programs, and some people have developed their "skills" at making sarcastic remarks. But we remember those hurts and they affect our kids' relationships to one another later in life. As a parent, I want to be the thermostat that sets the emotional temperature of our home, not a thermometer that just registers it. Requiring a compliment or even two to replace a snide remark is a good remedy for a sharp tongue.
- Put a stop to angry horseplay. Our boys loved to wrestle with one another at times. But when someone got hurt or tempers began to flair, I made them stop. My mother tells a story of two of her brothers who would wrestle and get angry. One day one of them stabbed the other. Thankfully, it was not

a life-threatening injury, but I refused to allow things to go that far in our home.

- Overcome perfectionism and criticism. A significant percentage of the population is made up of perfectionists. But perfectionism is a thing that varies from one person to another. There is no National Bureau of Perfectionism Standards. Perfectionism means that you have an internal standard of how things ought to be. Anything less rubs you the wrong way. Shining it on would violate your principles or create knots in your gut.

   So how can you live with things that are less than perfect? Gauge standards and expectations to ability for your child's age. Do not redo their chores for them. Show them how to do them better and let *them* redo them. Bite your tongue when you are tempted to criticize. Be more affirming of any little step in the right direction. Embrace the fact that others cannot be just like you. Enjoy the differences. Relax. Just as you want others to give you room to make mistakes and grow, extend that graciousness to others.

- Don't be afraid to apologize. You probably know people who *never* say they are sorry. Too bad for them. They probably have plenty of relationships that are wounded and damaged when they could be restored and refreshed. Your children (and other adults) know when you've blown it. It's not a secret. Putting on a façade of "having it together" is so phony, and even kids know it. Clean things up before they fester and ruin relationships and steal the joy you could have.
- Be quick to forgive. Forgiving doesn't mean the offender was okay in what they did. It just means you are letting them off the hook from owing you for it. You are turning the debt over to God for collection.

    A word about rebuilding trust and restoring a relationship after wounds. Restoration of the relationship is not automatically a by-product of forgiveness. It takes time and effort. Forgiveness is granted; trust is earned. The offender must show they have changed. John the Baptist asked for the Pharisees to produce fruits (actions) to show they had truly repented. Do not force yourself or others to be restored without the proper rebuilding necessary.

- Pay attention to the dynamics between your children. Do not allow one child to bully another in your home. Be aware of what is going on in all rooms at all times. Many adults were abused by a sibling while growing up, and they still bear the emotional hurts.

Expressing Love in Ways that Resonate

Just as dogs can only hear the sound of a dog whistle, people are tuned to different frequencies when it comes to love. Piano strings vibrate when certain notes are played that match those of the strings. Our hearts sing when someone does certain things for us that communicate love. In his book, *Five Love Languages*, Dr. Gary Chapman explains. Here is a small synopsis of my understanding of the languages.

- Physical Touch and Closeness – the need to sit close by or hold hands. The appreciation of hugs and physical tenderness. This is not sexual in nature, just human affection.
- Gift Giving – the joy of finding and giving just the right gift. It may or may not be expensive, but just says, "I thought of you when I saw this."
- Acts of Service – loving to do things for those one loves. It might be fixing things, providing meals,

- cleaning a room for the person, running errands for a loved one, or other benevolent acts.
- Words of Affirmation – building the other person up with compliments and admiring words. Buying greeting cards with just the right words. Calling to tell the person you love them and believe in them.
- Quality Time – taking time to interact. It might be playing a game or listening with great focus and attention to what the person has to say. Watching a movie together does not seem to satisfy this need as there is limited interaction.

When those we love and live with speak our love language in the most resonant ways, we feel touched and more satisfied. We observed that one of our children tended to get into more trouble if she had not had enough quality time with her dad. His work had him out of the house quite a bit, and she needed focused, intentional time with him.

Although my parents loved each other dearly, I remember some miscues in how they expressed it to one another. I remember my dad buying flowers for my mom, and her not valuing them like he wanted her to. Her top love language is acts of service. She made clothes for us and worked to decorate our home. She did entrepreneurial things to help our family. Dad's love language is gift giving. He grew up in the Depression, and his family struggled financially. He remembers questioning the love of his parents.

We discussed the love languages with our children. We asked what they thought each other's love languages were and what they thought their own were. Some were quite easy to tell. We ranked all five love languages 1 to 5 (most to least) for each person and posted them on the refrigerator. Then we encouraged the kids to try to express love to each other in those highest ranked ways at least once during the week.

When my husband's birthday comes around, I try to express my love to him in ALL the love languages. But I know what the most important ways are for him, and I make sure I cover those first.

Thinking through ways to make your home a loving one may be one of the most productive things you can do. Trying to do all this at once might be intimidating or overwhelming. Choose one or two things to work on at a time.

Analyze whether there is any behavior you are allowing that destroys the love in your home. Scripture talks about removing the little foxes that spoil the vines. It's the small things that define our homes. Be intentional with your targeting in these areas. Make yours a house of love.

Endnotes

Proverbs 13:24
Matthew 3:8
Five Love Languages: The Secret to Love that Lasts by Dr. Gary Chapman. Also versions on love languages of children.
Song of Songs 2:15

Chapter 7
The Importance of Marriage and the Home

One of the purposes of the home is to demonstrate kingdom living to unbelievers. It should show how powerful and blessed it is to belong to God. The Bible says that the home of the wicked is cursed by God, but the home of the righteous is pronounced to be full of blessing and joy and happiness. We also are teaching, by our example, how our children should live.

A Primer on Marriage

Central to the identity of the home is a good marriage, and a good marriage is really about partnership. From the beginning with Adam and Eve, married couples were called to work together. There are two extremes in our culture. On one end is the idea that women don't need men. Some women are so independent, they cannot work *with* their husbands. The other extreme is that of the woman who is so "submitted" she is passive. She has no thoughts of her own, she does not manage her home and her children.

Somewhere in the middle is a healthy place of partnership in marriage, with both spouses bringing the fullness of their gifts and strengths to bear on the work they have to do. If both spouses are aggressively supportive of each other, what a different picture this is from either of those extremes I described. Most of the time, you are both working toward the same goals. You are pouring your energy and strengths into each situation. You discuss what needs to be done, where you are going as a family, and you both agree. On the rare occasion that a couple cannot come to an agreement after a thorough discussion, submission then kicks in. Here is where a woman should yield to her husband's leadership. He bears a heavy responsibility to be careful in his judgment and decision making. She reminds herself not to be too ready to say, "I told you so," if he is wrong. You must keep working together.

Unconditional Love
The husband is to lead responsibly. He is to love and serve his wife as Christ did the church. This is a sacrificial love. Jesus gave his very life and his comfort up for his Church. A husband is to be a servant-leader.

    A good husband and father is nurturing. He should want what is best for his family, and work hard to bring that about. This actually goes beyond protecting and providing for a family. The idea of husbandry is that a farmer. A farmer cultivates the growth and development of his crops. He looks after the multiplication and health of his animals. Just as Jesus is the Vine and we are the Branches, a husband and father should see to the health, growth and spiritual condition of his family. He will be aware when things are stressed. He will call a halt and take everyone out for ice cream or a vacation when needed. He make sure hearts are matching actions with his children. He will set an example his children can follow and his wife can joyfully support.

Amazingly, Jesus loves unconditionally – even when we don't deserve it. This is a tall order for a human being, but definitely part of the job of husbands and fathers. This is something women crave and need from their husbands.

Unconditional Respect
Similarly, a woman is to give unconditional respect to her husband. (Ephesians 5) It's funny how women understand the need for unconditional love, but think husbands should earn respect. I believe God's commands in Ephesians 5:22-33 are not random. God knows what men need and what women need. Women want affection and caring and tenderness. Men need respect and admiration and

affirmation. When one or the other spouses withholds these needed things, the marriage is unhappy and unhealthy. And the Lord is not pleased.

My husband and I often recommend the book *Love and Respect* by Emerson Eggerichs. If you can attend a conference by the same name or watch the DVDs with a small group, seize the opportunity. After many years of marriage, George and I went to one, and it felt it was a piece that had long been missing in teachings on marriage.

Conflict Resolution

A stable marriage provides security for children. If your children hear you and your spouse arguing frequently, they will grow up wondering when the other shoe will drop and separation and divorce come to crush them. If your child is perpetually insecure, ask yourself if he or she feels their world is secure.

Sometimes we must enter the tunnel of conflict or tunnel of chaos, so to speak, in order to work through our issues. Just make sure you have your discussion in private, not in front of the kids. Harsh angry words, name-calling, swearing, and yelling are not necessary nor do they produce the desired results. Plant good seeds, reap a good harvest of kindness, patience and understanding.

Talk things through calmly or go for a walk to cool off, and *then* talk things through calmly. Be sure you pursue the issue and finish the job of discussion so that you come out the other side of that tunnel with a resolution and agreement. Get professional help if you need it. (Your insurance may help pay for counseling.) Fight for your marriage and your legacy.

Home as a Refuge

Home should be a refuge, a place where your family returns from the hassles of the day to find safety and peace. It should be a place where people are rooting for each family member's success. Parents must train this into their children. Having a refuge also means that meals are planned and timely. Bedtimes are usually on schedule. Expectations are clearly defined.

Home should also be a place where one is expected to learn and grow. It should be a safe place to make mistakes and learn from them. It means that kids are under control, not running amuck. The household should be focused on the family unit, not just one family member, especially not a crabby or tyrannical child.

Making Memories

Home is the place for making memories. Talk to your children about family history. Celebrate answered prayer. Rejoice together in accomplishments. You may want to write a one or two-word reminder of each on a smooth stone and keep it in a basket by your fireplace.

My children remember "M & M Parties" well. When one of the little ones was being potty-trained, we all had M & M's (and even called Grandma and Grandpa) to celebrate their success.

I treasure a story in my father's family about how a tornado in Oklahoma past through the family farm. Only a guitar was broken and a large tree uprooted. God protected them from the devastation that surrounded them. Share memories with your family that will support and build their faith.

We tell our children of a time when we were nearly out of food, and someone called and brought groceries over to us. It was an answer to prayer!

Intentional Parenting

Hospitality and Evangelism

Much of the early church was developed in places where there was no church building, but believers met in homes. Being hospitable is mentioned in the Bible as a must. If you are having company, you can prepare your child by explaining who is coming, what they are like, if they have children, and what you like about them. *Table Talk* by Mimi Wilson and Mary Beth Lagerborg is a good resource for conversation and hospitality ideas. I also like *The Mom & Dad Conversation Piece* by Bret Nicholas and Paul Lowrie. Try to have some of the food prep work done in advance so that the event is enjoyable rather than stressful for mom.

Compassion and Ministry

Several times throughout the last 37 plus years, my husband and I have had someone living with us. Once it was a single girl with family problems. Once it was a family coming off the mission field, needing to get their feet under them. For four delightful years it was my husband's great uncle, a retired cowboy in his late 80s. He was SO good for us as a family! In the New Testament, Priscilla and Acquilla invited a young minister home to teach him more about the Lord. What better place for these things to happen than in a home!?

We have hosted numerous small groups and Bible Studies. I have mentored young women. I've had ladies over to learn to cook or do canning. Needless to say, I didn't do much of this during the season of 5 toddlers, but in later years I was able to do more.

Teen Hangout

During our kids' teen years I made our home the place to hang out. We always had lots of decks of cards (they went through a phase of playing "Spades" for hours!) and food for snacks. Once our daughter brought a friend home with her after school. This girl's home was not pleasant or nurturing. She looked at our Crock-pot, which was plugged in and cooking our dinner and she said, "Your family is weird." How sad that such a small indication of nurturing was weird to her.

Home and the Holidays

Speaking of making it happen, nowhere is that more true than with the holidays. Women shop for gifts, plan elaborate meals, invite people over for parties and get-togethers, and pack the suitcases to go to Grandma's. We decorate and make sure no one is forgotten.

Intentional Parenting

Do you focus more on Santa or more on the birth of Christ? Is Easter more about the Resurrection or the Easter Bunny? Be sure to add Bible studies and symbolism to your holidays that will plant memories that stay with your children. My friend, Phyllis, lived abroad for many years. She was determined to plant seasonal celebrations into her children that would stay with them no matter where they lived or what path they chose in the future. Her book, *Celebrate the Seasons* is full of ideas and Bible Studies for doing that. Be sure your scrapbooks or photo collages include spiritual things during the holidays.

Tag-Team Parenting
My husband and I were a team when it came to parenting. We told the children, "Mommy and Daddy always agree," even when that meant we had to go talk behind closed doors before we gave them an answer. We came out of that room with a united front. Kids are notorious for pitting parents against one another. They will ask one parent for something and then go to the other parent if they don't like the answer. If you let that work for them, you will find yourself worn out and mad at your spouse. Your spouse will feel caught in the

middle, and the bad guy no matter what they do. Don't let the kids set you up!

Another way to be a good Tag-Team Parent is for each parent to back up the authority of the other. If a child is not listening to Mom, Dad can say, "Did you hear what your mother said? Respond to her when she talks to you." Mom can say, "Don't you ignore your father when he's talking to you." I once heard a speaker who told about how he learned as a child to manipulate his mother and his sister. He ruled the roost, pressured his mom and sister, and got his way regularly. That translated into a young man who knew how to get what he wanted from women. As a father, he was on the lookout for such behavior, and was stern with his boys if they gave their mother a hard time.

Taking Time to Listen

Everyone in a family needs to be heard. Whether it is the events of the day or the troubles of the heart, create a pattern where kids are heard. Introverts will have to be drawn out. Extroverts will have no problem talking. You may have to help the speakers take turns hearing each other out. Some people are internal processors, and prefer to talk about things after they have figured them out in their minds. Some need

Intentional Parenting

to talk *in order* to figure them out, or process externally. They may talk all around the problem before arriving at a solution and their final way of thinking about a matter.

If mom has been with the kids all day, how wonderful for Dad to take time to chat with kids and listen after dinner. Sit on the couch (without the TV on) and chat. Draw them out. Don't correct their expressions. Just let them tell you. This is not the time to "fix them." It is just a time to be heard and build the idea that you will listen to them in the future. Beware! If you go into "fix it" mode, they will be less likely to talk to you in the future. They will not feel safe in telling you what is on their minds. Save that for another time.

I believe that there are Dads who are good providers, but not good in building relationships with their kids. Take it to the next level, Dad, and develop that habit of listening and conversing with your kids. Mom, if you are the task-oriented, get-it-done person of the house, make time to gear down and be a listener. When your kids grow up, you will be thankful for the groundwork you laid for having a real friendship with them.

For some practical tips see the section on How to Be a Better Listener beginning on pages 283-286.

Feminism

While many women would not call themselves feminists, they carry some of the tenets in their minds. Feminism has become a part of the fabric of our culture.

I have done a number of amazing things, from politics to talk radio to founding two K-12 schools. I don't think anything has been as rewarding or as challenging as raising children. At the end of life, I'd rather have the company of my children and my family than the loneliness of the feminist ideal.

Feminism emphasizes the value of women working. It seems to think that women who do anything "less" are unfulfilled, bored, or simple-minded. And it ruins your figure! I believe that life has its seasons. During the season of raising children, parents must be tuned in and attentive. Careers can wait if it means kids get more adult input and attention. (For those single parents who must work and parent alone, you are living in a tough season. You are the ones who find ways to make it *all* work!) We made do with less money, simpler vacations, and less "toys" in order for me to stay at home with our growing children. Sure there were times that it was not as exciting as a job might have been, but I have never regretted the time I poured into our kids.

Intentional Parenting

Feminism underestimates the needs of children. They talk about children taking care of themselves and being independent. Recently I saw an article about teaching kids to "self-advocate," code for going to school officials for help, rather than expecting busy parents to go to school and straighten out problems. Kids need parents to oversee what is going on their worlds. They need to know parents will fight for them when it is needed.

Feminism pushes women to be stronger, even masculine. It downplays feminine virtues such as gentleness, patience, kindness and goodness. I believe that the pervasive vulgarity in our culture is a direct result of femininity being pooh-poohed. We need women who will stand up and say, "Mind your manners," and "Watch your language." We need wise women who are tender and nurturing and wise.

Feminism tries to say that our ideals of what is feminine and what is masculine is a result of how we are raised. They try to ignore God's design. He made women to be equal in value to men in the eyes God. Both are redeemed in the same way, both have the opportunity to have relationship with God. Yet he has given us differing assignments. Women excel at helping and completing their husbands and bosses. They are usually primary nurturers and correctors of children. Women change things. In the settling of the Old West, men blazed trails and conquered the wilderness. Women followed to bring civilization. Things began to change. They wanted law and order, they required schools and churches be built, they preferred wood floors and carpets to dirt floors. And the men were happier and lived better (and longer) as a result of feminine influence. Today's woman can raise the level of life for her family above mere existence.

It is important that parents embrace the seasons of child-rearing and legacy building. When possible, men must provide for their families so that mothers can stay home. Some women must work outside the home to make ends meet. Single moms have no choice. Still, every woman must make home a special place to be. Men can do this a little, but women really making it happen. Women, do not be afraid to invest your energies during this season. You won't regret it!

SPECIAL SITUATIONS

Single Parents

Many families are not living in a traditional two-parent situation. Single parents have significant challenges. They

Intentional Parenting

often have no one to share the load, discuss sticky situations with, or to tag-team off to when they tired or overwhelmed. They may also have ongoing conflicts with ex-spouses in parenting styles and decisions.

You may want to find a pastor or a grandparent who will back you up when things seem to be stuck between you and your child. Our single parent daughter had her dad available to help her in just that way. He could talk to a recalcitrant grandchild who just would not listen to mom. He would even give a swat if the child kept refusing to obey mom, but usually having a talk with "Granpy" was a big enough deal to do the job. As a pastor, my husband would sometimes have a talk with the children of a single mother in our church when she was overwhelmed, praising her for doing a good job and reminding the children to obey and respect her.

Another important matter for single parents is consistency in discipline and expectations. Our daughter, who was a single parent for eight years, said the most important tool in her parenting toolbox was consistency. She said if she let that slip, she was sunk.

Be sure to talk with your "ex" about parenting decisions. Tell them what you are doing and why. Ask them politely to consider following through on the same measures. You cannot dictate the other parent's choices, but a united front and consistency are priceless when it comes to giving children a stable upbringing. Hopefully, they will see the value of working together for the child's well-being.

Beware of children playing a parent and an ex against each other. Put a stop to manipulation by the child to get their way or to get more "stuff" out of you. Communicate with the ex about stories you hear about what happened at their house. (They may or may not be true.) Even the sweetest kids try this stuff. Help your child be confident that you staying ahead of any emotional games they might try to play.

Step-Parents
Step-parents may struggle with a seeming lack of authority. This certainly should be well-discussed and settled before a single parent remarries. You should have a thorough discussion about how you plan to parent together. It is also important to give children time to adjust to the idea of having a step-parent. Couples often force the idea of a remarriage on children before they are ready, and much trouble results.

Intentional Parenting

Once you are married, the driving principle, in my opinion, is the sanctity of your home. While in your home, the child must respect both the parent and the step-parent. Don't let the child pit you against each other. Both parents need to present that unified front to the child. Remember, have those private discussions when necessary. If a child is disrespectful to the step parent, the other parent must back them up and require the child to be respectful. The "ex" may suggest that the step-parent does not have a say so, and in legal decisions they do not. Similarly, your "ex" has no say-so about how things are done in your home.

In the day to day functioning and working together, in the trenches of obedience and disobedience, the step parent cannot relinquish this position of authority in his or her home. Even if things are done differently at the ex's home, you must require respect and obedience toward the step-parent while at yours. Do not speak negatively about ex-spouses within your child's hearing. This pits them against you or against your ex. Do not make them choose to love you and hate the other parent. No child should have to endure this kind of emotional tug-of-war.

In blended families, make sure step-brothers and sisters receive the same treatment and discipline. If there is not equality, there will be resentment and eventual rebellion. Make sure rules and expectations are consistent for all.

If your child is at another home part of the time, be sure to have a conversation about privacy and private body parts with your child. You cannot control who your child is around while at your "ex's" home, and unless something illegal is going on you don't really have a say. If you ever suspect your child has been abused while at under the "ex's" care, take your child immediately to a doctor and call the police if it proves out.

Living with Grandparents

At times single parents may find themselves living with grandparents whether for financial reasons or for temporary housing difficulties. As grandparents who has had adult children and grandchildren reside with us for a number of years, we emphasized that we were not substitute parents or built-in babysitters. We let the parent correct the child. If something came up while the parent was home, we referred it to them. We did everything we could to convey our respect toward their role as parent. We wanted to fulfill the role of grandparents and enjoy our grandkids. While we did provide a roof over their heads, utilities that were not in danger of

Intentional Parenting

being turned off, and a refrigerator full of food, we did not buy diapers or formula. That was the parent's job. We did not intervene in behavior situations unless asked. We were affirming of the parent in front of the child.

If you are a custodial grandparent, you must fulfill the parental role. You might prefer not to do so, but the child needs a parent first and foremost. Read and implement the parental strategies throughout this book.

Deployed parents

Since I live in a city from which many military people deploy, I have seen first-hand how difficult this is for families. Do all you can to stay in touch and keep your spouse informed on the stages of your child's growth and the challenges of parenting you are going through. Skype, email, or employ any means at your disposal to stay in touch frequently. Talk to your children about what to expect with transitions before and after deployment. Transitions can be hard. Both the military and Focus on the Family have great resources for assisting your family.

Adoptions, Foster Care

Intentional Parenting

Parents who are called to adopt and to provide foster care are amazing. Our son and his wife have done so, and this situation has special challenges. When possible, try to get good health history information. Some parents have had surprisingly difficult challenges that would have been easier if they'd know health problems ahead of time. Be a part of a support system where you can get encouragement and even a respite for the ongoing load you bear. Get professional counseling when needed. Above all, pray and ask the Lord for guidance in understanding what is going on in the hearts of these precious children. It may change the path you need to take in dealing with their problems.

Use caution about having older children care for younger children. Give each child the benefit of being trained by an adult. Allow older children time to be children, not substitute parents.

Unbelieving Spouses
Scripture says that if a spouse is an unbeliever, let them stay (reside) if they are content to do so. It says that the unbelieving spouse may be won over to faith if the believing spouse is a good example and not pushy. I highly recommend Stormy Omartian's *Power of a Praying Wife* (or

Intentional Parenting

Husband) for anyone who is dealing with this. Do your best to work together in partnership in your parenting even though you may not attend church together.

On the other hand, if your spouse is abusive to you or to the kids, GET HELP NOW! Call a counselor, call a pastor. Do not allow this for the sake of a roof over your heads. Protect your kids and yourself. Read *Boundaries* by Cloud and Townsend. Put distance between yourself and the abuser until they agree to calm down and get help. Do not believe the lie that it is your fault, or that if you do what they want, they will change. True love does not cover for this bad behavior. It gets help – for both the abuser and the abused.

Endnotes

Proverbs 3:33
James 1:19-20
Romans 12:13; 1 Peter 4:9; Hebrews 13:2
Acts 16:14-15
Acts 18:24-26
Love and Respect by Emerson Eggerichs.
Celebrate the Seasons by Phyllis Stanley. www.nutritionalbreadbaking.com.
1 Cor. 7
1 Peter 3
Focus on the Family, 1-800-A-FAMILY keeps a referral list of Christian counselors for many cities throughout the country.
Renewal Ministries of Colorado Springs www.renewalcs.org

Intentional Parenting

Chapter 8
The Anger Remedy

Many people grow up believing anger is synonymous with discipline. It is what they experienced as a child. Perhaps they don't know any other way to make their children mind them. It does not have to be so. And you don't have to live with the guilt that anger brings.

Set Yourself Up for Success

First of all, anger makes discipline about *you*. The focus is not on the child's behavior, but you screaming. It takes over the situation. Kids tip toe around to avoid setting you off. Stop. Think about things. Why am I angry? Did I set myself up to be this way? Did I warn the children that if they did such and so, I would be angry? What other action could I choose? Is this even about their behavior?

Planning ahead in your mind helps keep you from setting yourself up. Think through some common behavior problems you deal with and come up with a plan for what you will do to respond (other than flying into an angry outburst). If you must warn the child who is headed toward trouble, tell them what you will do.

Intentional Parenting

Calmly explaining the negative behavior of the child and the resulting consequences (with firm follow-through) is much more powerful than having the situation break down to you freaking out and yelling. So to set this up, I might say, "If you do x you will earn the consequence of y. It's your choice, but I don't think you want to go there." This makes discipline about their choices, not your rage. This is much more productive in training them to think before acting.

Additionally, I never threaten; I only promise. And I keep my promises. So I had to be sure that the consequence was one I would carry out. Silly phrases like, "I'm going to hang you up by your thumbs," are worthless. You're not really going to do that. Choose a consequence that is appropriate, in keeping with the seriousness of the offense. One swat for hitting a sibling is fitting. Five swats for hitting is too much, over the top. Leaving the table without dinner is appropriate for a child who refuses to eat what is put in front of them. (No snacks or food until the next meal.) Force feeding a child is not appropriate. You could ground them from TV, but a consequence related to the offense is more effective. Don't threaten anything if you do not plan to follow through!

Why are you Angry?

There are several ways to look at your anger. Ask yourself *why* you are angry. My husband who is a pastoral counselor says there are three main causes:

Anger = A-H-E-N

- Hurt
- Expectations (unmet)
- Needs (unmet)

Review and consider these. Analyze what's going on inside your head and heart. Walk through the AHEN acronym in your mind. Are you actually upset about something else unrelated to your child's behavior? When you realize what is really bothering you, don't take it out on the kids. Address what needs to be addressed separately from dealing with kids' behavior problem.

Consider if you have communicated your expectations and needs to your children. For example, if you are getting ready to go somewhere and you are in a hurry, don't yell at the kids to hurry up. Explain that you forgot to set the alarm and now the time is short. You need them to grab their shoes and coats and get to the car quickly. You are bringing breakfast for on the road. End of story; everyone is moving in the same direction.

Intentional Parenting

How often would our lives be more peaceful if we took time to think through and explain to our family members what is going on? Don't set yourself up!

If you are over-tired or PMSing, bite your tongue. Address the real issue. Don't take your weariness or hormonal instability out on others. I used to have one day a month where I either fought rage or ridiculous fear. Either I was seething or I was sure my husband was going to die on the way home from work. I didn't even like being around myself on those days. And issues around the house that were real issues were blown out of proportion on that day. I learned to bite my tongue for a day (and taught my girls to do so also). It was better than cleaning up the mess my words would have made. And real issues could be addressed on a day when I was feeling better.

Many people grew up with adults who were angry and abusive. If you have serious issues from your past or unresolved conflicts that are feeding your anger, consider going to a counselor to help you work through the pain. My husband also recommends *The Anger Workbook* by Les Carter and Frank Minirth in his counseling practice.

Intentional Parenting

When Children are Angry

There is a history of violent anger in my family, so when our first child was about 18 months old and he began throwing toys all over his room in a rage, I was scared. I turned to the Bible looking for answers on how to direct him so he wouldn't grow up in this family pattern. I found the great scripture in Psalm 4:4. Back then we used the King James Version and it is stuck in my head: "What time I am angry, I will speak to myself on my bed." So I had my little son lie on his bed and talk to God about what was upsetting him. He could communicate with us, but in a calm way. We used this again and again over the years and it worked.

Angry Words

When people are angry or hurt they often communicate in hurtful ways. Yet psychologists tell us it is unhealthy to "stuff" our concerns and hurts. Where is the good balance for these difficult situations?

Scripture says we are to control our tongues. Our words can be like arrows piercing the soul of others. I found the most helpful picture of how to handle saying hard things in the example of the virtuous woman from Proverbs 31. It says the law of kindness rules her tongue. I taught my kids

Intentional Parenting

that they needed to communicate with one another; they needed to talk about problems and hurts. But the key is that they needed to use kind words to do so. They had to have those difficult conversations, but they needed to do it with kind words. They could not shred one another verbally. They could not "vent". Many times I would say, "Kind words only." They might roll their eyes, but now that they are parents I hear them saying the same thing to their kids.

When someone offends you or hurts your feelings, or if they are doing something that bothers you, you have to let them know. Rather than stuffing your feelings deep down inside, but you can choose the words with which to say difficult things. Frankly, stuffing things just puts them away until they blow up later from the suppressed pressure. Use words that build up relationships rather than tear down. I think this is a good explanation for "Be angry and sin not." Tell the truth. Be firm and clear. But do it kindly.

If hurtful, angry words have been spoken by your children, require an apology (see chapter 14 "The Correction Process"). Have the child practice using better words that are appropriate. For example, an annoyed child might say the terrible words, "I hate you!" when what they needed to have said was, "Please stop tapping me again and again. It is

Intentional Parenting

annoying." Help your child come up with appropriate words for their situation. This also instills the skill of thinking before they speak, and choosing accurate words to express themselves.

Temper Tantrums

I think temper tantrums personify the "Terrible Two's" in most people's minds. Children may become frustrated about their abilities or those that are not well developed or they may want their way so much that they are willing to scream for lengthy periods of time, kick their feet, and even may bang their heads on the floor to get it. You may feel like an emotional hostage to their anger.

    First of all, do not let their crying distress you. Pull the plug on the emotions of all this. Make this about them, not about making you (and everyone else in the house) miserable. Secondly, give them the opposite of what they want. Show them that this behavior will not give them what they want. For example, if the tantrum is to gain attention, put them in their room and tell them they can come out when they are done with their fit. If it is to get their way about food or naps or anything else, DO NOT GIVE IN. The behavior that gets rewarded gets repeated.

If you are in a store and they are pitching a fit to get something, leave it on the shelf, give them a discreet pinch and tell them to be quiet. If the crying continues, leave the store and take the discipline measures you need to at home. You can politely say to a store employee, "I'm sorry, I need to leave my cart and take this child home. We are working on this."

If you can stay peaceful in the face of their frenzy and continue to train them to proper behavior, you will win eventually. Here is one more place to embrace the hard work of parenting. Then reward yourself with a long soak in a bubble bath with a book and some chocolate.

Endnotes

The Anger Workbook by Les Carter and Dr. Frank Minirth
James 2:5-11
Proverbs 12:18, 15:4, 18:20-21
Proverbs 31:26
Ephesians 4:26

Chapter 9
Starting with Family Goals

Much of who our children will be as teens and later as adults is established when they are small. Experts say it is by age 5 that personalities are established. Much behavior is ingrained before children go to school.

Some parents abdicate their responsibility and leave it to someone else to teach their kids, perhaps eventually when they go to school. They wait to address problem behavior, or fail to do so consistently. Some default to what is popular in our culture at the moment.

This is like taking a boat out to sea without setting a course. If you let the wind and the current take you wherever it wants, you will end up lost at sea or smashed on the rocks. How can you take control of the ship of your family's future?

Beware of adopting goals that are only because that is always the way your family has done things. That's a little like the obedience "because I said so" mentality. Some family traditions are not based on solid principles or godly ways from scripture. Some practices are outdated and don't make sense to your kids. Make sure you know the reason why things are important as you create your family legacy. Train in things that will be of lasting value.

Start with Goals

Rather than start our parenting with correcting what we don't like, let's identify qualities that we do like. These are things we want to training into our children. Write out your list. What's important to you? What do you want your kids to be known for? For us it was:

- Loving and serving the Lord
- Finding answers to life's difficulties in Scripture
- Christian Worldview
- Honesty
- Obedience to parents with increasing personal strength to walk their own walk wisely
- Hard work / Good work ethic
- Family recreation – especially camping (made possible by a willing and hard-working mother!)
- Love of reading (I read aloud to the kids nearly every day and on long trips.)
- Having a well-rounded education, from how things work (engineering) to appreciating all kinds of music

Intentional Parenting

My daughter-in-law has added teaching her kids to laugh and be joyful. I tend to be rather serious, so I like that! I'll go into more detail in later listing specific skills I believe children need to learn at various ages.

After setting goals we had to think about how we would impart these things. In turn, that drove decisions about what kind of schools they would attend and what kind of churches we would be a part of. As you can see, our list was not very extensive or descriptive to start with. But it was a start. Over time, we added qualities to our list. (More about Christian character in Chapter 11.)

Basic Behavior

To start with, there are a few simple rules that are necessary to life.

- Obey parents. Parents, have the child's best interests at heart.
- Respect authority. This is a vital key to success at all stages of life. If authority figures are wrong, question them respectfully, including parents. (Parents must back one another up on requiring this. If a child is disrespectful to one parent, the other should call them on it.)

Intentional Parenting

- Live by scripture. It is our authority.
- Treat other people as you wish to be treated. That means with respect and consideration.
- Learn to do all you can for your age and abilities. Get knowledge, get skills that will be useful in life, get understanding of how life works.
- Be responsible for your things and your actions. Accept responsibility for what you've done. Parents must model this.
- When we mess up, we apologize sincerely. We try to make right and restore what we can.

For young children I like *21 Rules of this House* by Greg Harris. It is simple and straight forward. We had it posted on the refrigerator for our children. Parents must confidently require good behavior of children. And they must consistently model it as well. For small children, you *are* the self-control until they learn to have their own self-control.

Behavior in Public

To start with, behavior in public shouldn't be vastly different from what is required at home. Simple courtesy, how we talk to one another, and knowing the difference between "inside voices" and "outside voices" covers quite a lot. If your child thinks they must behave completely differently at a public event from how they do at home, your home standard may need to be reviewed. There are unchanging principles of human behavior that work almost everywhere.

Beyond that, set your child up for success by talking to them ahead of time about what the event will be like. Tell them how you want them to behave. For example, at a wedding, they must be more quiet than usual and sit still during the ceremony. Explain that and that you will be there to honor the bride and groom. It is their special day. If they are prone to saying "Oh, yuck!" at the kissing parts of a movie, warn them that when that happens in the ceremony they must hold their comments.

If you are going to a friend's house to play, remind them to ask for permission to go play with the other child's toys and to wait to be invited to go into other parts of the house. If a discipline situation arises, remove your child to a private place to handle it. Deal with problems frankly. Do not put the feelings of a friend over justice with children.

Correcting to the Family Standard

Once you have identified what your family goals are and what basic behavior is desired, you have created a family standard.

Intentional Parenting

You can correct your child to that standard. It is good to say, "In our family, we do thus and so. We do not do such and such." This helps children understand when other families choose different (perhaps lower) standards. If they are members of the Churchill family, it does not matter what the standards are for the Wellington family. Making these expectations clear for all members of the family help prevent knee-jerk reactions to offensive behavior.

Rewards vs. Bribing

In the real world, we are not rewarded for everything we do. We do many things just because they need to be done. Chores are a part of necessary life in a family. Everybody does their part, according to their ability.

Rewards and treats are good for extra jobs or things accomplished beyond normal requirements. A child who must be bribed for good behavior or basic chores will have a very hard time functioning in the real world.

Allowance (money) can be given as a regular thing, but make sure basic responsibilities are met prior to handing it out. Try to simulate real-world experiences that will help your child in the future.

Intentional Parenting

Individual Goals for Each Child

While on some level behavior standards and expectations will be the same for your entire family, you still have to deal with each child's natural abilities and quirks. Proverbs says, "Train up a child *in keeping with his natural bent,* and when he is old he will not depart from it."

First consider what your child's personality is. If she is melancholy, she might need to work on being joyful. If he is shy, he might need to work on how to make friends and how to communicate with small talk. (More on this in chapter 17.) Consider strengths and weaknesses. Look at ways to help them work on those – to reinforce strengths, to affirm talents – and to overcome weaknesses. Weigh what the next step is in each of the following areas for each of your children:

- Spiritually – Our priority was to work toward them having their own quiet time of Bible reading and prayer. Oh, how I wish I'd learned this before I became an adult! To follow up, I asked them what they were reading and what God was speaking to them about personally. I offered to get them a new devotional book if they needed it. We also encouraged them to respond to the Lord in spiritual matters at the level where their understanding was.

We encouraged their spiritual growth and development.

- Character – Consider strengths and weaknesses (see list in Chapter 11). Pick one or two to work on, perhaps for the next year. This is not really separate from spiritual things, but needs its own attention.
- Socially – How is the balance of being with friends and still treating family members well? Are they happy and positive in both settings? Are they able to carry on a conversation with people of any age, not just peers? Can they function comfortably in various settings? How are they at making and keeping friends?
- Academically – In what do they need to improve? Do they need a tutor or do you need to meet with a teacher? How can you help them get from here to there in their academic development?
- Physically – Are they active enough? Do they like to eat healthy foods? Do they need something to help with large or fine motor skills or controlling their energy levels? (We used a small trampoline for our hyperactive child to expend energy. Two of our girls

were a bit clumsy, so we had them take ballet to improve their muscle control.)

- Talents – Do they have an outlet for it? Keep things in balance and don't let love for a talent take over your life. Are chores and relational responsibilities staying in good order also? Are they ready to explore something more? Are they learning that talent also requires discipline, that developing talent takes hard work?

Setting family goals will help make parents aware of what they want to work toward, not just tackling negative issues. During childhood Jesus grew in wisdom, in stature and in favor with God and man. Our kids can too.

Endnotes

Ephesians 6:1 and the Ten Commandments (Ex. 20:3-17)
Golden rule: Matthew 7:12 and Luke 6:31. See also Leviticus 19:18, 34
Twenty-One Rules of This House by Gregg Harris:
  http://greggharrisblog.blogspot.com/2009/12/21-rules-of-this-house-by-gregg-harris.html
Proverbs 22:6, Amplified Bible
Luke 2:52

Chapter 10
The Uniqueness of Each Child

Scripture tells us that God has made each of us uniquely. We each have different fingerprints, different features, different personalities, and a different destiny. The Bible says God knows us, even while we are in the womb. In the miracle of life, He decides whether He needs a child to be a boy or a girl according to that destiny.

Girls tend to be more nurturing and more tenderhearted. Boys tend to be more rambunctious and adventurous. While parents may get frustrated with their child's personalities and quirks, we need to remind ourselves that we just may need more understanding of God creative design in our child.

Hopefully the ideas in this chapter will start you on a quest for more information in these areas.

Personality Profiles

If you are an extrovert, but your child is an introvert, you must help them out of shyness but not demand that they be like you. Some of our problems and conflicts with our kids come from the differences in our personalities.

Intentional Parenting

Years ago, we attended a seminar using DiSC personality profiling (now called the Classic DiSC). This one has been most helpful to me over the years. Some people like Meyers-Briggs or Kiersey-Bates tests, still others like the 4 animals explanation used by Gary Smalley or the four temperaments (sanguine-choleric-melancholy-phlegmatic). You can find great resources online like www.discprofile.com or www.16personalities.com.

Knowing your family members strengths and weaknesses really helps in parenting and in marriage. You can avoid pushing someone's buttons and setting off negative reactions because they feel threatened. For example: are you (or your child) an introvert or an extrovert? Introverts prefer to be alone. They weight their thoughts and actions inwardly. Extroverts are more people-oriented. Introverts may be drained after being with people. Extroverts will feel charged up after being with a group of people.

Some people (including children) are external processors. They need to talk things through to figure them out. They don't want you to draw any conclusions about the discussion until it's over. They may even take different positions throughout a discussion, then settle on one at the end. Other individuals are internal processors. They need to think it through and figure it out before they want to talk about it. Some people need time to adjust to change. They are more security-oriented. Others like change and action. They may have more of a desire to be in charge and directing things.

You're the adult, so as a parent it falls to you to understand and adapt to your child's needs. You must identify the potential weaknesses and help them learn to compensate for them. At times you may feel annoyed by their needs and differences, then guilty that it bugs you. If your personality is like theirs, your challenge is to help them overcome things you also deal with. I love the conversation between the parents in the movie *I Remember Mama*. The Swedish Dad says of one child, "Ja, she is the quiet one," and of another who has just run out of the room in tears, "Ja, she is the dramatic one."

Giftedness

As much as educators have been aware of special needs children who struggle to learn, they are becoming aware of the needs of gifted children. The goal in either case should be to take a child from where they are to the highest level possible for their abilities. Beware of schools that use gifted

Intentional Parenting

students to tutor other students rather than focusing on encouraging them to learn at a higher level themselves.

Books like *Seven Kinds of Smart,* and *Emotional Intelligence* look at different kinds of giftedness. Here are the areas to consider:

- Verbal / words
- Musical
- Visual/artistic/mind's eye
- Athletic/body awareness/movement
- Math/science/engineering
- Social/people
- Spiritual/self-awareness/internal/self-analyzing

Parents must keep a balance between challenging, yet not pressuring, their child to achieve, especially in their areas of giftedness. We must allow them time to be children, and not push them too quickly. Children who might be academically capable of skipping a grade in school might not be ready to handle the social and emotional pressures that go with that.

Be sure to give your children unconditional love. Don't let yourself give more approval or seem to love them

Intentional Parenting

more when they perform or achieve. You can rejoice, but affirm *who they are* aside from what they achieve.

Learning Styles

Parents must also be committed to being savvy education consumers. Much has been written about different learning styles:

- Visual learners – learn by seeing, both in pictures and in print. This is the most common way schools function.
- Auditory learners- learn by hearing. Better at memorizing information if they make a recording to listen to.
- Kinesthetic learners – learn by doing; "hands-on" learners; must be moving or touching to engage their brain.

I believe parents should help choose their child's teacher. Consult with the head of the school you are considering to see if they will let you be a part of that process. Make sure the teacher can work with your child's learning style in an effective way. Ask about lead teachers who are coaching new teachers in these areas. One smart teacher I know lets wiggly kids stand and wiggle in the back of the room while she is conducting a lesson. The child has to be quiet and stay engaged with the class, but their need to move is satisfied.

Shop for programs at schools that fit your child rather than trying to make your child fit the school. Most cities allow students to choose the schools they want to enroll in if parents will bear the burden of transportation to get them there. You must also be well-informed as to the content of the programs. Some gifted programs treat children different, training them in humanistic ways to solve the world's problems. Make sure the school's worldview is not focused on one-world globalism or undermining your Christian values. This is especially true with college programs. Many children have lost their faith in humanistic colleges and universities. Even some Christian colleges have professors who do not believe in the virgin birth or the authenticity of Scripture.

Spiritual Gifts

Spiritual gifts are for children too. The list in Romans 12:6-8 becomes evident in our children given time and the opportunity to participate in serving others. One child's mercy heart may be obvious as they take in strays and help their friends. Another's tendency toward the prophetic might be manifest in their strong opinions about things being black and white, never grey. Consider not only the gifting, but also the weaknesses or dangers associated with imbalance. A person who likes to do benevolent work or help in areas of practical service might do so to the detriment of his or her family's needs. Help your child moderate their tendencies.

Large Families and Single Parents

Some large families are the best ever at discovering and encouraging their children's individual gifts. We often treated our five children as a group, but we did several things to help them as individuals. We let them be in different activities. I took only one at a time grocery shopping with me. They got $3 to spend (in the 80s and 90s) and could have all my attention throughout that time. They usually talked my leg off. My husband occasionally took them on individual "dates" to get an ice cream cone and talk.

Be careful that you are not having your older children raise your younger children. Each child needs your care and input. Kids can help with chores, but correction, training and affirmation must come from parents. If older kids tend to boss younger ones, remind them that you are the parent, they are the brother or sister. A child raised by a sibling cannot be trained to the higher level that would come from an adult. So often "first born" children are easily identified because they are more responsible and better trained. Give each of your children the raising of a first born.

Adopted Children

Adopted children have special needs and challenges. Hopefully you are able to get good health history information. Sometimes abuse and neglect imprint devastatingly negative things on a young child's psyche. Much can be overcome with lots of prayer and love, but it is a big job. Embracing the uniqueness of each child and then their additional issues will be important to their success and yours.

At times it may be necessary to get professional help for your child's issues. Doing so is the smart thing to do, not a negative reflection on you.

Endnotes

Job 10:8-11 and Jerimiah 29:11
Jeremiah 1:5 and Psalm 139:13-16
DiSC Personality Profile. See also www.16 Personalities.com
Please Understand Me by David Keirsey and Marilyn Bates
7 (Seven) Kinds of Smart by Thomas Armstrong
Emotional Intelligence by Daniel Coleman
Discover Your Child's Spiritual Gifts by Don and Katie Fortune

Intentional Parenting

Chapter 11
Character Training

Character, whether good or bad, is defined by actions and attitudes deep in our hearts and minds. Proverbs says even a child is known by his behavior. No matter how much a person might *want* to be like someone else, her own choices determine what she *is* like. As a parent, we have the opportunity to form those attitudes and build a foundation into our children that will lead them to be responsible and caring adults.

It starts with your example. Children watch and mimic their parents. If your children are more than a year old, you've probably seen them do something just like you, sometimes to your chagrin.

Who should we compare ourselves to? Who is the standard? Of course there is always someone less capable, less competent, less good. And there is always someone better, say Mother Theresa.

Actually, Jesus is the standard. God wants us to be like His Son. That's a tall order. Teach your children that this is a life-long journey, and that you are still working on some things. God planned for his children to become more and more like Christ, his son. I love the Scriptures that say our desire should be to please God, to make Him happy. Ditto for our children wanting to please us. It is a natural and healthy response to love.

Distractions and Defeat
The enemy of our soul and of our children does NOT want to see us serving God and becoming more like Christ. He hates us and he hates God. He will send all kinds of circumstances and people to fight against us. He will tell your children lies, whispering in their ears that you are against them or don't love them. You must be intentional and determined in your work for spiritual development in your children.

Start with family prayer and Bible reading. A family devotional time helps everyone grow together rather than separately. Talk about the sermon from church or extend the topic from that time by looking at it more deeply. Talk about how to apply spiritual truths in a personal way. (If you don't know how to do this yourself, consider the *Life Application Bible*.) Pray together about concerns your family has. Share what you are praying about with your children. Talk about when prayers are answered.

Intentional Parenting

Discuss current events at the dinner table or as you drive in the car. Look for Scriptures that explain how to think or why things are the way they are. Deuteronomy 6:7 talks about this as a requirement for a blessed life.

Character Goals
Second, consider the areas you put down for both family goals and individual goals in the area of character. Looking at strengths and weaknesses, what do you need to work on? Are there one or two big things you want to emphasize for the next 6 months to a year? Or do you want to work on a certain trait each month? How will you go about that? Here are some ideas:

- Find scriptures to memorize about the trait (See list in Appendix 2).
- Find books and other resources from the library and stories that illustrate the trait. Aesop's fables are one source. Another favorite in our family are the *Adventures in Odyssey* CDs and DVDs from Focus on the Family. There is also a wonderful radio program or you can listen online. These programs depict character matters in an interesting and exciting story format. If you need more ideas try *Books That Build*

Character by William Kilpatrick & Gregory and Suzanne Wolfe or *Core Virtues* by Mary Beth Klee. Bill Bennett has published several different levels of *The Book of Virtues*. Ask your librarian for help in finding books that exemplify the virtues you are instilling.

- Talk about ways to practice the trait. Explain what it looks like in everyday life. Then do it. One year, in the charter school I ran, we were emphasizing the traits of service and generosity near Christmas time. I asked the principals of our schools to come up with a way to show this trait toward the neighboring schools. (Each had a regular public school next door.) The principal at the middle school / high school had the kids take cookies to the staff at the nearby school, and tell them Merry Christmas. They were quite surprised.

Character Education by John Heidel and Marion Lyman-Mersereau is a source used by teachers. These two volumes have a calendar with activities planned for each day of the month. You may find some ideas from other religions in the books, but you can choose to ignore those.

Intentional Parenting

- Have your children make a poster about the definition of the trait. Post it in the dining area for all to see. (Or download ours at www.IntentionalParenting.us.)
- Read biographies of famous people who exemplify the trait. Discuss Bible characters as examples.
- Consider rewards or at least be sure to praise when your child acts out the trait you are working on. "Catch" them doing good things.
- Find more traits and ideas at www.values.com.

Two-Year Plan

The following is a two-year rotation I used at a school I founded and ran. Our emphasis on Character Education and working well with parents made our school exceptional.

Year One

August / Sept. – Respect & Responsibility
    Courtesy
    Deference v. Rudeness
    Obedience v. Willfulness
    Attentiveness as a responsibility
    Citizenship
    Dependability
    Wastefulness
    Orderliness
October – Integrity & Honesty
    Sincerity

Intentional Parenting

November – Gratitude
December – Compassion & Generosity
    Availability to help others v. Self-centeredness
    Hospitality
January – Curiosity & Alertness
    Initiative
    Discernment (not the same as judging) – *One person taught me that you must judge the actions of others, but never the value of the person. That is God's job.*
February – Persistence & Diligence
    Endurance
    Determination
March – Loyalty
April – Patience
    Gentleness
    How does pride feed impatience?
May – Joy & Enthusiasm

Year Two
August – Respect
    Courtesy
    Deference v. Rudeness
    Obedience v. Willfulness
September – Responsibility
    Dependability
    Wastefulness
    Orderliness, organization
    Attentiveness as a responsibility
    Citizenship
October – Integrity, Honesty
    Sincerity
November – Gratitude
December – Compassion & Generosity

Intentional Parenting

      Availability to help others v. Self-centeredness
      Hospitality
January – Humility
February – Leadership & Courage
      Sacrifice, Duty
March – Self-Control, Self-Discipline
April – Gentleness, Kindness
      Do nice guys finish last?
May – Wisdom

Character Traits in Correction

Third, when you correct children, talk to them about not only what they did wrong, but about the trait they need to put on instead. When you see behavior you don't like, look at the following list and identify the positive behavior that should replace it. I love the list from Bill Gothard that follows here. Correct the bad behavior, the talk about and have the child practice the good behavior instead. And of course, you may find some *you* need to work on.

Character Trait List

Positive Trait	Negative Trait	Scripture
Truthfulness	Deception	Eph. 4:25
Alertness	Unawareness	Mark 14:38
Self-Control	Self-Indulgence	Pr. 25:28/ Gal. 5:24-25
Wisdom	Natural Inclinations	Pr. 9:10

Intentional Parenting

Resourcefulness	Wastefulness	Luke 16:10
Orderliness	Disorganization	I Cor. 14:40
Attentiveness	Unconcern	Heb. 2:1
Obedience	Willfulness	II Cor. 10:5
Hospitality	Loneliness	Pr. 18:1, Heb. 13:2
Reverence	Disrespect	Pr. 23:17-18
Discernment	Judgment	I Sam. 16:7
Thriftiness	Extravagance	Luke 16:11
Initiative	Unresponsiveness	Ro. 12: 21
Sensitivity	Callousness	Ro. 12:15
Sincerity	Hypocrisy	I Pet. 1:22
Generosity	Stinginess	II Cor. 9:6
Diligence	Slothfulness	Col. 3:23
Faith	Presumption	Heb. 11:1
Contentment	Covetousness	I Tim. 6:8
Responsibility	Unreliability	Ro. 14:12
Justice	Fairness	Micah 6:8
Virtue	Impurity	II Pet. 1:5
Joyfulness	Self-Pity	Pr. 15:13
Thoroughness	Incompleteness	Col. 3:23
Discretion	Simple-mindedness	Pr. 22:3
Punctuality	Tardiness	Eccl. 3:1
Humility	Pride	James 4:6
Compassion	Indifference	I Jn. 3:17
Boldness	Fearfulness	Acts 4:29
Flexibility	Resistance	Col. 3:2
Dependability	Inconsistency	Ps. 15:4
Love	Selfishness	I Cor. 13:3
Tolerance	Prejudice	Phi. 2:2
Decisiveness	Double-mindedness	James 1:5
Gentleness	Harshness	I Thes. 2:7
Forgiveness	Rejection	Eph. 4:32

Intentional Parenting

Availability	Self-Centeredness	Phil. 2:20-21
Security	Anxiety	John 6:27
Creativity	Underachievement	Ro. 12:2
Cautiousness	Rashness	Pr. 19:2
Determination	Faintheartedness	II Tim. 4:7-8
Deference	Rudeness	Ro. 14:21
Persuasiveness	Contentiousness	II Tim. 2:24
Endurance	Giving Up	Gal. 6:9
Patience	Restlessness	Ro. 5:3-4
Enthusiasm	Apathy	I Thes. 5:16, 19
Gratefulness	Ingratitude	I Cor. 4:7
Loyalty	Unfaithfulness	John 15:13
Meekness	Anger	Ps. 62:5

Endnotes

Proverbs 20:11
Romans 8:29
2 Corinthians 5:9; Colossians 1:10
Ephesians 6:12
John 10:10

Character Trait List, pp. 113-115 reprinted by permission, Institute in Basic Life Principles. www.iblp.org.

Chapter 12
Teaching Respect

Respect is consideration we grant to others. It includes admiration and esteem. We make a choice about to whom we show deference. Children cannot be a law unto themselves. They are not the smartest nor the most important person in the room. Do not create a monster by letting your child think everything and everyone should revolve around them. Who and what should children be taught to respect? Here are some important categories:

Respect for Parents and Adults
Children must start with respect for adults. Certainly they need to respect parents. That is part of the Ten Commandments. It is repeated in the New Testament. (We'll talk about obedience later.) Do not allow your children to get away with hitting you or speaking disrespectfully to you. Do not allow them to ignore you or stall in obeying you. This isn't about stroking your ego; it's about what is good for them. Remember, what you *allow* is being trained in.

Intentional Parenting

If one parent sees the other being disrespected or ignored by the child, the observing parent needs to provide back up and call the child into account immediately.

Children should respect grandparents and older adults. We preferred to have our children call adults by "Mr." or "Mrs." If the adult was a good friend we allowed them to address them by their first name with Mr. or Miss attached, Mr. George or Miss Tiffany as they do frequently in the south. Some adults want to be called by only their first name. They are trying to be friendly and approachable. We insisted on maintaining our standard of using Mr. or Miss because respect was important to our training.

Another way we showed respect to those who are older is by serving them first when there was a dinner. In our child-centered society, children are often served first, but how much more fitting to take care of the elderly first. Teach kids to move cautiously around those with canes, walkers, or wheelchairs. They may be able to run hither and yon, but they could knock down a fragile adult in the process. Another way to show respect is to visit your older relatives, even if they are in nursing homes. Listen to their stories. Enjoy their past experiences. Be inspired to become the kind of older person who will leave a legacy to others. I have learned some very valuable lessons from my elderly family members.

Incidentally, I would say to adults, **speak to children with respect**. Extend to them the *utmost respect*. Sometimes adults talk better to their dogs than they do to their children. This is shameful. Even corrective words should not be harsh and angry. They should convey your disappointment or frustration, but they should focus on what is the goal – the good of the child and their growth. You can be firm without being disrespectful.

Respect for Authority

Another thing children must respect is authority. Authority is put in place by God. Criticism of government and elected officials is part of our culture, but it is not right for Christians. The book of Jude connects it with the wicked. Peter says not even angels do that.

Do you make it a habit to criticize your boss in front of your children? Do you talk negatively about your pastor? Scripture says that even slaves are to honor their masters! That goes for bosses too.

There will always be someone over our children, whether in school or in a job. Even someone who owns their own business must obey laws and pay taxes. If you do not teach them to function under authority, you are doing them a huge disservice. I have a number of years working with food pantries and ministries for the poor. We helped many people who could not keep a job. Some had become homeless or came to us for help year after year. One common denominator I kept noticing is a lack of respect for authority. Set your child up for success by teaching him to respect authority.

The Apostle Paul shows us how to deal with unjust or ungodly authority. Paul rebuked a man who struck him, but then apologized when he found out it was the high priest. He proceeded to use wisdom and insight to argue his case. He was respectful even toward someone who was not acting right.

What about Contrarians?

I am concerned for those who pride themselves in being contrarians. They like to fly in the face of accepted wisdom and authority. Any accepted wisdom is to be challenged. It's good to think for yourself and not to be a robot without thought, but to disagree no matter what, to enjoy disturbing others just to shake things up seems to me to be connected to rebelliousness. And the people I've known who are rebellious are stuck. They frequently do not seem to mature beyond the point at which they decided to be rebellious. They do not seem to grow in wisdom. If your child is contrary, always saying no when you say yes, you must work on this. Do not allow this to stay in their heart. Help them find a good balance of respect for the wisdom of others and being allowed to have their own thoughts and ideas. Teach them to test their ideas and not think they are fine only because they are their own.

Respect for Peers and Siblings
In our self-focused world the Bible takes a very different view of how to live. It says we are to consider others as more important than ourselves. Just as Jesus laid aside His status in heaven to come to earth for us, we are to have a humble mindset. We are not to think of ourselves more highly than we should. There is so much in scripture about working as a group for the good of one another, about each part being necessary to the other just as the various parts of your own human body must work together and be valued.

Teach kids that that other person is precious to God. God created them the way they are, even if their ways bug you. Respect is a good part of the Golden Rule: Do unto others as you would have them do unto you. (For more on Sibling Rivalry, see page 205.)

How to Raise a Narcissist

I remember reading in the 80s that we were raising the "Me" generation. Recently, I saw the cover of a magazine proclaiming this the "Me, Me, Me" generation. We all have probably dealt with someone who was beyond selfish, who was narcissistic – self-centered, self-focused, and willing to do whatever it takes to get what they want. How would you raise a child to be like this? (Tongue-in-cheek, of course.)

- Make sure you teach this child the world revolves around them. Other people must adjust if necessary to accommodate them and be supportive. After all, they are cute, they are smart, and they are so interesting. Everyone should appreciate them.
- Never let them know how much you sacrifice for them. They should just expect this, right?
- Give them everything they want. Don't make them earn things.
- Don't inconvenience them with your requests that they do chores or come to the table when you call.

Tell them you will wait until they are finished with what they are doing.

- Make sure they are always the center of attention. Let them draw attention to themselves no matter what the occasion or location.
- Don't honor another child's birthday without giving this child a present also. You wouldn't want them to feel bad.
- Get other children to adjust to this child's wants whether it's what to play or whether to share. It's such a little thing. And your child's ideas are good.
- Intervene so this child is not corrected by teachers, scout leaders, or others. Some people are just negative and out to get your child.
- Put this child's feelings first. Making them happy is your goal in life. Being healthy and productive will work out somehow.
- Don't acknowledge the excellence of others. Your child's work and talents are the best. They should have won the talent contest or the art contest or the music contest. The judges were biased.

- Never let this child experience consequences. Shield them from all difficult things in life.
- Never be negative or corrective. Do everything in only positive ways.
- Don't tell your child no. Whether they are asking for stuff in the grocery store or pleading to go out with friends you aren't sure about, give in.

Of course, you don't WANT to have a narcissistic child, let alone deal with an adult who is this way. Practice the opposite of the above actions. Respect for others, care and concern for others, and honest correction is like sunshine to the dark germs of selfishness.

Respect for the Property of Others

Another way to apply the Golden Rule is to respect the property of others. If children are allowed to drop trash anywhere, that is disrespectful. Who will clean it up? The trash fairy? That property owner must clean up their yard or the next hikers in the forest will have to put up with or clean up your child's mess. Not okay!

If a child breaks something at someone else's home, they should inform you and you should offer to replace it. Then help your child earn the money to help pay for the item.

Intentional Parenting

Treat the home of a small group leader with respect. Offer to help tidy up before you leave. My heart cringes for the woman who found permanent marker on her white carpet after her Bible Study group left. She knew the parents must have seen it and said nothing. How rude!

Similarly, if you are the host it is appropriate for you to expect others to respect your home and belongings. If a visiting child made a mess, I had cleaner spray and rags handy to allow that parent to help clean it up. Even though it is a bit uncomfortable, I think this respects the dignity of all persons and helps those who are untrained in how to walk out respectfulness in other's homes.

We had separate toys for our home group. We did not require our children to share everything. We did say that if they brought out a toy, it had to be shared with others. We respected their dominion over their belongings.

With regard to sharing with siblings, you might want to allow a child to have one special toy they do not have to share unless they want to. This gives them some "private" ownership while encouraging sharing overall. It also helps the siblings to learn to respect others' boundaries by having to ask to play with that special toy.

If you borrow something from someone, be sure to return it cleaner and in better condition than when you got it. God made laws in the Old Testament about what was to happen if you borrowed your neighbor's ox and it died while you were using it. If you can't afford to replace it, don't borrow it.

Some people expect to be able to borrow whatever you have. We have learned that we only loan what we can loan with a clear conscience, even if it is not returned. We do not loan expensive items like our camper for example, because if it were damaged we could not afford to replace it. The borrower likely could not either. These are things that God has given us and we are responsible for them. It is our choice to give when and where we feel led. It is inappropriate for someone to expect us to give just because they want what we have.

Respect for the Things that Belong to God
Respect for the things that belong to God starts with creation. I love the beginning of Psalm 24: "The earth is the Lord's and the fullness of it, the world and they who dwell in it." In my mind this is a soaring statement! The majestic mountains and all the tiny bugs are His. The oceans and the

fish and the krill. The minerals and chemicals with which we make our inventions. The people and the minds of the people that invent and build. It's all His. I give thanks that I was born with hands, with a good mind, and in a free country.

One of the ways we taught our children to be respectful of creation was to leave nature better when we left than when we found it. We taught our kids to pick up trash and clean up our camp or picnic sites. As human beings we have dominion over creation. We can use it. But we must be responsible with how we use it. We don't worship creation, but we appreciate its beauty as a gift from God. Isaiah wrote that God could have made it a wasteland, but instead He formed it to be inhabited. God could have given us something like Mars and said, "You're fallen. Make do." But in his love He gave us waterfalls and forests and geysers and islands. This is abundant evidence of His love! (Not to mention coffee, chocolate, and all the other things that grow into the foods we love!)

We need to respect the Word of God. It has come to us at great cost. The consistency and validity of it are more real than the documentation we have on major historic figures like Julius Caesar. It is inspired by the Holy Spirit and useful for our growth and correction. My mother wouldn't let us set anything on a Bible. What a good example of giving special honor to the things of God. Once while preaching in Ukraine, my husband slapped his hand on his Bible for emphasis. Later the pastor of the church explained to him that that was offensive to those in his culture because they felt it dishonored God's Word.

Recently, the *Passages* traveling Museum of the Bible came to our city. (They plan to open a permanent museum in Washington, D.C. in a few years from this writing.) If you get a chance to visit this in any city, don't miss it! It is amazing. This is a great opportunity to learn about the history of the Bible and the price many people paid to give us the Bible in our language. Raise your children's awareness and appreciation for God's Word. Read more at www.explorepassages.com. (I LOVE their lectures as well! This is a great resource for older teens.)

We need to respect the church. God chose it to make known salvation and his multi-faceted wisdom. He chose the "foolishness of preaching" to make the gospel known.

We should also honor those in ministry in the church. Paul said we were to hold them in affectionate esteem. Unfortunately there are those who have brought dishonor to the church and to the name of the Lord. Let God and church authorities deal with them. Speak frankly with your children about those who fall, but we all need to remember humans are imperfect. Only God is perfect.

Those Who don't Deserve Respect

What about abusive parents or grandparents? Should we respect them? What about those who are dishonorable or have committed heinous crimes? At minimum, we can be polite. Teach your children not to speak angrily or disrespectfully. We are not to be overcome by evil, but to overcome evil with good. That doesn't mean you have to entrust your child to be babysat by family members who might not treat them well. (See Chapter 4 Parenting Pitfalls and Unprotective Parents.) We are to be wise as serpents, yet harmless as doves. If a grandparent is harsh and demeaning, make sure you are present with your children at all times when they are around this person. This includes protecting your spouse from your family if they do not treat him or her well. Do not sacrifice your family to conventions (like being together at Christmas) or expectations of others (like spending the night or going to Grandma's for two weeks by themselves).

If a family member tries to influence your children and twist their thinking into accepting a false view of what is right and wrong, do not allow your child to be around them. If they try to make your children feel sorry for them when they are actually reaping what they've sown, manage or remove contact with that person. You decide what is safe and permissible for your children. Explain to your child privately how you see the matter. Don't apologize for protecting your child from injury or lies.

A friend of mine had a family member who was homeless. He tried to manipulate the family into housing him, but he was involved in drugs and alcohol. He called their Christianity into question because they wouldn't invite him to their home. They helped him get a placement into rehab, but he wouldn't go. Rather than have him at their home, they offered to buy him dinner at a restaurant. He tried to get the kids to feel sorry for him, playing on their emotions. The parents had to cut off contact between him and their children to protect them from being confused. They did the right thing.

Another friend of mine had been abused all through her childhood. It was not safe for her to see the offender, even as an adult, because of unresolved issues that put her in an emotional tailspin. How can she honor her parents as Exodus 20 commands? She can refrain from denigrating them, even though they might deserve it. She should not lie about what happened during her childhood in order to protect them. She should not shine it on and put it behind her. She can make sure they never lack for food or shelter, but provide it at arm's length. She can make sure they are in a decent nursing home when they are old. She can honor their position as parent, even though she cannot honor this person for who they are.

What NOT to Respect
Do not give equal respect to other religions. Our society is very pluralistic. That means they think that all roads lead to heaven. Wrong. Jesus said no one comes to the Father except through him. Deuteronomy 28 is full of the differences between choosing God's way which is *filled* with blessing, or going against His way which is full of dryness, loss, slavery to sin and death. Jesus died for your sins. You cannot work your way to happiness. There will be a Judgment Day. God doesn't agree with pluralism. Be polite to individuals, but do not accept falsehood.

Intentional Parenting

Do not respect other people's sinful or bad choices. Our culture says something is okay for someone else, but not for us. The Word of God puts forth absolute truth. Explain to your children *why* sinful choices are bad. What will be the likely consequences of that choice? How does God feel about it? You know that things do not come out the same over time. Whether it is things that are a matter of right and wrong according to Scripture (like lying, living together, stealing, etc.) or things that are not healthy (like smoking or gluttony), God's word is clear that there are consequences.

Do not respect bad kinds of government or evil rulers. Again, due to our pluralistic thinking, our kids may be taught in school that communism or socialism are acceptable choices for government. Explain how dictators and those who violently oppress their people are abhorrent to God. God hates corruption where rulers enrich themselves at the expense of their people. Holy Wars and Jihad is not pleasing to God. He also hates when justice is perverted or when only the rich get justice.

Do not respect political policies that are immoral. Truth is worth fighting for. Abortion (killing unborn babies still in the womb), euthanasia (so-called mercy killing), assisted suicide (for the terminally ill), and infanticide (killing babies) is wrong. So is embryonic stem cell research using aborted fetuses. In a way these are sacrifices to the gods of convenience and willfulness. They are ways to avoid consequences. And those who use it for financial gain will have to answer to God.

Do not respect money or those who are wealthy more than those who are not. Justice should not work better for the rich. We should not show preference for the wealthy. We should give care and attention for widows and orphans. The Bible calls this true religion.

To some extent what we give respect to defines us. Make sure that you are respecting things that are good and that you are speaking honestly about things that are not worthy of respect.

Endnotes

Exodus 20:12; Ephesians 6:1
Leviticus 19:32; Proverbs 20:29
Proverbs 8:15; Romans 13:1
Jude 1:82 Peter 2:10; 1 Timothy 2:1-2 Fear God, honor the King...
Ephesians 6:5
Acts 23:1-5; Exodus 22:28
Philippians 2:3-4
Philippians 2:5-8

Intentional Parenting

Romans 12:3
Exodus 22, 23 and other verses
Acts 5:4
Psalm 24 and Psalm 50:10
Romans 1:25 says worshipping creation is a sign of a decadent society.
Isaiah 45:18
Timothy 3:16
Ephesians 3:10
1 Corinthians 1:21
1 Thessalonians 5:12-13
Galatians 6
Romans 12:21
Matthew 10:16-17
John 14:6
Proverbs 28:4
1 John 3:17; James 1:27

Chapter 13

Requiring Obedience

One of the Ten Commandments states that children are to honor their parents. The New Testament restates that as obeying parents and reminds us that it is the first commandment with a promise. Until they do this on their own parents must **make their children mind.** Recently during a Sunday school class on parenting, I said this to the parents, and there were a few there for whom this seemed to be an "Aha!" moment. Yes, you must *make* them mind!

Why Obey?

I think parents sometimes hesitate to require their children to obey because they are afraid they will look like a dictator. They do not want to be bossy.

First of all, there is the matter of protecting the child from harm. You must train them to stop instantly when they are reaching for that electrical outlet, or pulling pots of hot soup off the stove. Very young children do not yet understand "cause and effect". This is part of *you* being the self-control until they learn some.

Certainly, scripture mandates that children obey parents. God knew what he was doing, what was needed for the good of the race. Rather than requiring obedience to feed your ego, you are training them for their own good. You are setting them up for success in life.

Learning Curve

Secondly, when you require obedience you are paving the way to being able to teach them greater things. If a child is disobedient and full of himself, how can you teach them anything? They will not listen. From a young age you can train them to be teachable.

Babies will learn to eat on a routine schedule and sleep at night. They will learn to crawl and then to walk. Toddlers will have a bit more self-control and will be ready for potty training somewhere around ages 2 or 3. They will have the ability to pull their pants up and down, to be aware of when they need to go, and to be able to communicate well enough to tell you it's time. You can then begin to work with them on taking care of business consistently. It would be silly to expect to watch over and control that for them for the rest of their lives.

Intentional Parenting

Normal growth and development means your goal is to train your children in such a way that they need less and less of your control. As they get older they become more able to do things without being told and to make good decisions for themselves. (See Chapter 17 for a list of skills to work on at various ages.)

Your mindset needs to be like this graph similar to one from Richard Fugate's *What the Bible Says about Child Training*, with children's ages going up the left side:

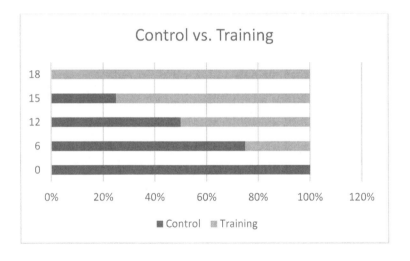

Again, the younger they are, the more you have to be in control of their behavior and their activities. But while they are young, until they can do it on their own, you ARE their self-control. As they get older, they should become less and less dependent on you to control them. At the same time, the level of difficulty and amount of things you can teach them about increases as they become older. The best-case scenario is that they are fully capable and fully independent of you by the time they leave home (well, almost). I think it is interesting, and probably accurate, that somewhere in the "tween" years (around 10-12) things should even out about half and half. This is not exact or scientific, but you get the idea. As the child's ability to control themselves goes up (and your need to control them goes down), his ability to receive training and learn new things also goes up.

If this change is not occurring over time, the child is not becoming capable. If the adult is not gradually releasing control, the relationship is not healthy. You can see how controlling parents handicap their children. I'm not sure if they envision suddenly releasing their child, but if so, the child will not be ready. A gradual process is better.

When you become aware of how much you are really responsible to train your child, it may be daunting. Parents may wrongly believe that their work and involvement lessens with the teenage years. They look forward to things getting easier, to being able to check out or do what they want to do other than parenting. The pattern I have just described puts a heavy burden on the parent to invest time and energy in order to teach those higher level skills. If you don't, you'll be bailing your young adult out of various predicaments, fixing things for them, and spending nights worrying about them. Imagine the teenager who drives a car, but never learns to check the oil.

Like so many lessons in life, it's cheaper to learn on the front end than after a big mistake. I am sad for adults who struggle, struggle, struggle – all for a lack of training. By being intentional, you have the opportunity to give your adult kids a leg up on life.

Communicating

When you are talking to your child about obedience or what you are instructing them to do, be sure you are making eye contact. Help them focus on your face and eyes. Do not let them look everywhere other than at you. You may want to ask them to repeat what you have told them to do. Make sure they understand before you move on to something else.

Intentional Parenting

Bright children

One pitfall for parents is in knowing their children are super-smart. They are so amazed at the child's brilliance, they make the mistake of letting the child lead the parent. Often they let them do what they want. This child is set up for being "wise in their own eyes" by having too much independence too soon. How much better to have a grown-up in charge, training them how to live. If you weave self-discipline into them, they will be able to use their intelligence so much better. Most of us know someone who is very smart, but not disciplined enough to make anything out of their life or talents.

Arguing

Children sometimes proceed to argue rather than obey. You must stop this immediately. Do not get drawn into an argument about something you have told your child to do or something you have said they may not do. This is often a tug-of-war about your authority or their laziness. Analyze what is really going on and address it.

Parents who allow their children to argue may doubt themselves or want to be kind and pleasant rather than commanding. Choose your battles. If you don't want to be firm about it, don't give the order. It's better not to tell them they can't do something than to do so and then change your mind.

The one caveat here would be to allow discussion or explanations (not arguing) when the child is giving you information you might not have, for example in a discipline situation. Be sure you are judicious in these moments; make sure you get the whole story before pronouncing a judgment.

Consistency

Our moods change from day to day. Our family standards and requirements should not. Kids should be able to count on what was a no-no yesterday is still a no-no today. The TV show that was off limits last week is still off limits this week. Children should not have to tiptoe around the house, wondering when a parent will explode in anger, never sure whether the requirements today will change because mom is in a bad mood.

Being consistent takes discipline and training on the part of the parent – disciplining *ourselves*. WE are the hardest part of the job. Often in the midst of raising children, we are confronted by our own weaknesses and problems. And that can really affect whether or not we are consistent. You may have to overcome some personal weaknesses while you are working on your child's.

Age Appropriate Requirements

What you require of a 13-year old is obviously more than what you require of a 3-year old. Sometimes young children do goofy, immature things. In an older child, the same behavior would be foolish or dangerous. Make sure you think before you react to either. Is it immaturity or misbehavior? Consider how much you have (or have not) talked about this issue. Have you explained the dangers and the consequences? Does the child actually know what you mean? My friends had been working with their four-year old on obedience for some time. One day, the child said, "Dad, what does 'obey' mean?"

When the Child is Tired

Getting involved with a behavior battle when your child is tired and it is past their bedtime is just setting yourself up for frustration. Set yourself up for success by having regular bedtimes and making it early for the little ones. If Junior missed her nap and is out of control, put her to bed. Don't

Intentional Parenting

let her terrorize the whole household. You can tackle the behavior issues when they come up the next time.

Making a child obey is not about satisfying our need to be in command. It's about training a child's life toward adulthood. Our focus is preparing them for the future. Good parents require obedience as a part of the course of growth and training, leading to adult independence.

Endnotes

Exodus 20:12
Ephesians 6:1-2
Proverbs 26:12; Rev. 3:17

Be sure your child crawls! More and more learning disabilities are tied to skipping this step in development. It builds neuro-pathways in the brain because there is a balancing motion between left hand and right knee, right hand and left knee. Put away that walker and let them crawl. If your child missed this, go to www.DianneCraft.com for exercises that help in rebuilding that skill.

Chapter 14
The Correction Process

Correction is something that we must do for our children. It is one of the least fun parts of parenting, but the Bible says it is part of loving our child. It is necessary for the molding of their character and for the maturing of their thinking. Every year, in every community, we hear of young people in fatal car accidents with extreme speed and alcohol involved. Correction may save your child from danger and perhaps even an early death.

The apostle Paul corrected the church for its mistakes. He said he was not sorry for doing so, and that their godly sorrow would lead to real repentance and change.

Correction is not about taking your frustrations out on the child. It is not about getting even with the child for what they have done. It is not even making them pay for what they've done. It is something you do *for* them, not *to* them. Correction is part of training them for how to live life as an adult. You are using correction to show them the error of their ways and teach them better ways, opposite choices.

Discipline or correction should be a first response, not a last resort. By addressing issues as soon as they arise,

Intentional Parenting

you make the situation about the child's behavior, not your displeasure. If you are getting angry, you have waited too long to address the problem.

Remember, you are FOR your child. Do not allow misbehavior to make you dislike them. Continue to show that you value them. You are both in a process together, training them up to be good and wise. You are setting the stage for them to be capable, successful adults.

Correction may involve giving them a talking to, a swat or two, making them stand in the corner, or taking away privileges. For teens, you may ground them or have them write a paper on the correct behavior that needs to replace what was inappropriate.

Steps in the Correction Process

Before you jump in and start correcting your child, consider these steps that need to occur:

- Make sure you have the whole story and are informed about all the parties who were involved. Take time to get the facts. Proverbs says one person seems right until you get the other person's story. How true!
- Make sure you are not lashing out in anger or embarrassment. If you are too wound up, delay the

Intentional Parenting

consequences. Tell the child to wait for you on their bed until you calm down. Let them stew while you cool down. If you discipline in anger, you'll be in the wrong, not them. And they'll know it. Don't breed resentment in their hearts. Keep the focus on their behavior, not your frustration.

- Give the child a warning if this is the first offense or something you are newly training them about. Further discipline may not be appropriate at this time. This is part of setting that tone that you are for them, and that you are working on this process together.
- Choose your timing wisely. Young children must be corrected quickly, before they forget what happened. Older children may need to have a talk with a parent a bit later if others are present. One example would be dealing with an offense at a child's own birthday party. Unless it is serious or likely to cause an emergency, talking to the child after everyone leaves might be more appropriate.
- If this will be more than a few words of admonishing, move the discussion and discipline to a private place. You may need to go into the bathroom or to their bedroom. Do not embarrass children in front of

siblings or friends. Correct in private. Praise in public.

- Ask yourself, is this willful disobedience? Or is it a childish mistake? Is there intent to harm another person? These factors will change how you address the problem.
- Ask yourself – is this something for which I have trained a standard of behavior? Does my child understand the moral reason why this is wrong? Are my expectations age appropriate?
  1. **If YES** – confirm that they have violated the family standard or standards of the Bible. Consider what Christian character trait has been violated. Look at the opposites list on pages 112-113.
  2. **If NO – you cannot discipline the child for doing what you have not taught them to be wrong.** Perhaps this will require adding a new topic you've not previously addressed. You can discuss this thoroughly, but do not punish at this time.

- Weigh carefully, have I promised particular consequences for this? If so, you MUST follow through. Do not make empty threats.
- Explain to the child that the discipline is **their choice**. If they do right, they will be blessed. If they choose to disobey, they are choosing the consequences. Do not let them think this is something you are doing TO them. You are just carrying out the effects of their choice. They have chosen this. They have earned this.
- Don't say, "You always…." Or "You never…." This can create hopelessness that change is impossible. It's probably also inaccurate. You can remind the child if this is a repeat offense, but let them know you expect this to change. You don't expect to be dealing with this over and over.
- Make sure they understand the feelings of those they have harmed. Make sure the relational side is discussed. Most behavior problems are not just about chores. It may also be about offending someone else or making extra work for Mom. Be sure this is a part of the discussion.

Intentional Parenting

- Be sure you administer discipline with firmness, and without anger or apology. If you are giving swats have them bend over. If you are taking privileges away, begin immediately and be clear about how they may be earned back or when the grounding is to be over. Do not use lengthy time periods for young children. It will lose meaning.

  If spanking, make sure wiggly children are held firmly so that you do not swat their back, only the tush. If our toddlers were thrashing when it was time for a swat, I would sit on the toilet, hold their legs between mine, and bend them over with my left arm, giving the swat with the paddle in my right hand. For toddlers you may need to remove the diaper. (One of my children tried putting multiple layers of underwear on to create extra padding when they knew a swat was coming. I had to go laugh in my room out of their sight after I caught them!)

- Allow the child to cry (quietly), but not to scream and make everyone else in the house miserable. Not allowing them to cry would be unnatural and unhealthy.

- Lead the child in a prayer of repentance. They need to tell God they are sorry. Make sure the child is truly sorry, not just sorry they got caught. Godly sorrow leads to repentance and change. Explain that repentance means to go the opposite way next time. Talk about the correct character trait that you want substituted in the future. Make sure they understand what that looks like. Explain the put on – put off process you want to see happen.
- Lead them in apologizing to whomever they have hurt or harmed. Enforce this. Have them say, "I'm sorry. Will you forgive me?" If they refuse, you are not finished. You have more work to do explaining what is right and what is wrong with their behavior. Have you known people who NEVER apologize? Don't allow your child to develop that pattern. Make sure they look the offended person in the eye and speak clearly. Then the offended person must say, "I forgive you." If they won't forgive, you must deal with that. Remember, forgiveness is just letting go. It doesn't mean what they did was okay.
- Consider whether restitution is necessary. If something was broken or damaged, talk about how

- the child can earn money to replace the item. If something was stolen, take the child back to the store manager or person who owned item to return it and apologize.
- Restore and reaffirm your relationship with the child. Hug them. Tell them you love them. Do not withdraw nurturing. Overcome evil with good if you are offended. I love how God deals with us when we mess up. Psalms says we fall, but are not utterly cast down. He doesn't throw us away or give up on us.
- Let the issue go. Let the child start fresh. Do not let resentment build. Love keeps no record of wrongs done to it. Don't bring up past issues every time you deal with the child. Don't keep a mental list. This does not mean you do not watch for improved behavior, or make yourself unaware of tendencies. You just give the child the opportunity to act new, to have no judgments stacked against them. You do not carry a grudge against them.

Discipline Ideas

Scripture embraces the idea of spanking. Some in our culture do not. It is not illegal, but it is wise to limit swats to one or two and never more than five. This is not a tool to convince or change your child's mind or personality. Some children are still not convinced you are right, even after swats. You would be abusive to keep spanking, trying to break their wills. And spanking doesn't work for everything. We used it primarily for deliberate disobedience or for if they hit someone. Dr. Dobson says not to use your hand, but something inanimate like a paddle or wooden spoon. I agree. This helps prevent confusion about hands that caress vs. swatting. The most important thing is NOT to spank out of anger. Dispense corporal punishment firmly, but without anger.

Families that are doing foster care usually cannot spank. The state stipulates this. This is something to consider before you decide to do foster care if you have other children. Remember these children often *have* been abused. You must be careful to separate your ways of disciplining from that. Their perceptions of discipline are crucial to your success in training them up for a good life. Several of our friends went through the foster-adopt programs and one of our children has. These adoptive children were actually relieved when the year was up and adoption was complete, because now they could get a simple swat and have the discipline be over, compared to grounding and other methods that dragged on.

Time-outs are a popular way of disciplining, but you seldom see them being effective. I think they are more useful as a warning, a chance for a child to stop what they are doing, consider where things are headed *before* they get in trouble. If a child gets in trouble for being over-active, they can help him refocus and discipline himself to slow down. Small children can handle a time-out for about as many minutes are they are years old. If you set the time for too long, a small child will forget what this is all about.

As a punishment for any behavior (usually to avoid spanking), time-outs work poorly. They are easily ignored by the child as ho-hum and no big deal. And a big caution: sending teenagers to their rooms often only gives time for them to build resentment and stew about supposed injustices. Do not use this as a frequent punishment. You may have better success with having them work with you on a project or chores.

Consider having the child practice the opposite of what they were after. If the misbehavior was to get out of work, having to do extra chores might send the message that the behavior does not work out like they hoped. If they don't do their dishes because of laziness, more chores are in order. (I used to say, "You must need more practice!") If they do a poor job cleaning the bathroom, I call them back to do it right as many times as needed. ("Ooooh, yuck! Just look at the base of that toilet! Gross!) They'll get the message that it is easier to do it right the first time.

If a child treats family members badly, showing a preference for friends, then more time with family is in order and less time with friends. If insulting words were spoken, make them give compliments. If a child speaks disrespectfully, have them stop and try again with appropriate words.

When the children would run through the house, I would stop them and make them go back and *walk* the same path through the house. (More practice!) How much better this was for her than a spanking to get them to remember to walk.

<u>Natural consequences</u> are what adults experience. If you don't do your checkbook, you will have checks bounce and have to pay overdraft charges. Nobody spanks you, but the consequences do the job. Making a child delay their meal because they have not fed pets would be appropriate. For children, not being able to play until chores or homework are

done is a similar idea. You don't have to nag them, just let their desire to go play push them to do their work. If they leave their stuff lying around, put it in a "Butler Box" and charge a chore to get it back. Work for work. Four items, four chores.

One day I called my teenager to come get her coat which she had left lying on the couch. She came down the stairs, put it away, and went back upstairs. I waited. Then I called her back downstairs to get her shoes. Same process – down the stairs, up the stairs. Then I called her back a third time to get her book. In frustration she said, "Why do you keep calling me to come downstairs?! I'm getting tired!" I said with a smile, "If your stuff was put away I wouldn't have to." She got the point. She picked up everything else of hers that was lying around and took it upstairs to her room.

I remember having my <u>mouth washed out with soap</u> for lying when I was small. I used that for bad language with my kids. Another mom who is conscientious about chemicals uses vinegar. Obviously, this makes a real impression.

My philosophy was to make it SO not worth it to disobey. I made sure the <u>consequences were heavy enough that it was better to obey</u>. One mom made a child stand in the corner because he didn't do the dishes. Meanwhile, she loaded the dishwasher. Afterward, she realized he won! He still didn't have to do the dishes. Don't do that. Make consequences a bummer.

If a teen doesn't come in by curfew, a good natural consequence would be to move it up so they can be home by a safe time. Our weekday curfew was 11 PM. (Friday night and Saturday night was 1 AM for our near-adult teens. The bars close at 2 AM and I didn't want them driving when the drunks were out in force.) Calling at 10:50 to say they were on their way didn't count. They had to be in the house by 11. If they couldn't make that, I offered to move it up to 10:30 to help them out. (This would not mean that they were in by 11. I MEANT 10:30 if I moved it up to 10:30.) If that didn't work, we would try 10 PM for a couple of weeks. They made sure they were in by 11 PM. I don't think I ever had to actually move it up. They knew I would do it.

Our children had to pay for their own car insurance. (They might as well get used to it – they'll have to pay it for the rest of their lives if they drive.) If they got a ticket they had to pay for the increase that affected our entire policy. Even our teenage boys soon figured out that was a bad thing. If they were horsing around with the car, they lost the use of the car for a couple of weeks. Consequences that are tied to the offense are more effective.

Cautions

Here are a few things to think about to evaluate your discipline measures. First, make sure the consequence is enforceable. Do not threaten to make them stand outside without their coat because they did not hang it up. You won't want to carry that out and have a sick child. Don't set yourself up for something worse than the original infraction.

Secondly, don't do anything that is mean or that would wound their spirit. Embarrassing a child or just plain getting even is wrong and contrary to the nurturing we are to give as parents. If you feel guilty, don't ignore it; apologize.

Remember this is a process. Big lessons may take several episodes. Explain, but do not be disappointed if it takes more work, more situations for them to be convinced. This is part of the work of parenting. You train, retrain, and correct to the standard as often as you must until they get it. That's parenting. That's love.

Do not use multiple punishments for an infraction. Don't ground them from TV for a week *and* take away their music *and* give them a swat. That is over the top. You might be mad enough to do all that, but you don't want to sow the seed of wounding into your child's heart it would cause. That would be unjust.

Make sure the punishment fits the crime. You wouldn't make a child sleep on the floor for not making their bed. That's too harsh. You might have them make several beds next time (to practice!) You wouldn't refuse to allow a child to eat because they didn't do the dishes. You might have them do the dishes more frequently instead.

Be sure that your consequences are not too light. Children should get the idea that it is not worth it to disobey. If you find yourself dealing with the same thing again and again, your punishment may be too light. One of my now-grown children recently said, "Yeah, I was good, because you made it SO not worth it to disobey!" I smiled to myself and said, "Good!"

One last consideration: do a mental check to see if you are setting a good example in the area your child is struggling with. It's hard to see our children copy us. It's harder to discipline them when they do. Don't set the stage for your child to call you a "Do-as-I-say-not-as-I-do" parent.

And if you're having a bad day, have PMS or are just plain grumpy declare amnesty and let it all go. Go out for lunch. Pull the plug. Put *yourself* in time-out. Take a nap. It's better than wounding your children's spirits.

The Correction Process is a necessary part of training our children for adulthood. If you see it as a part of that, you will be more willing to invest the time and energy, to embrace the hard work of parenting.

Teach your children that obedience to God's way will lead to a blessed, happy life. You are happy and they are happy when they are obedient. Explain that disobedience brings sadness and pain. It leads to an unhappy life and lots of trouble and sorrow. The sooner they get this, the better their life will be.

Endnotes

2 Corinthians 7:8-10
Hebrews 12:5-9; Proverbs 23:13-14
Proverbs 18:17
2 Corinthians 7:10
Romans 12:21
Psalm 37:23-24
1 Corinthians 13:5
Isaiah 1:19

Chapter 15

Understanding Rebellion

The dictionary defines rebellion as an act or show of defiance toward an authority or established convention. When a child rebels, they are saying in effect, "Not your will, but MINE be done." In a sense, they are putting themselves above your authority. They are saying they outrank you. Obviously, you can't allow that to happen. What will this look like in five years? What will this look like as teenagers? How will this work at a job for when they are an adult? These questions should give you the gumption to tackle the battle of rebellion.

In the Bible story of King Saul, he had been ordered to destroy everything after defeating an enemy. Saul deliberately disobeyed God's orders. He kept some spoils of war. He tried blaming others. He made excuses. But bottom line, he didn't obey. Samuel, God's prophet didn't buy any of it. This famous story gives us the frightening scripture, "Rebellion is as the sin of witchcraft; stubbornness as idolatry.

Again and again throughout scripture, the nation of Israel was seen to rebel against the Lord. Each time they reaped bad consequences. They were defeated by enemies

Intentional Parenting

and taken into captivity. Twice they were reduced to cannibalism just to survive. God called Israel a "house of rebellion." Psalm 50 is a litany against their disobedience. God even says (my paraphrase), "You have done these disobedient things and I was silent. So you thought I was altogether like you. But now I'm coming and will show you that I am not!"

What do we see in the life of Jesus? He said our love for him is demonstrated by our obedience. Scripture says that Jesus *learned* obedience through what He suffered. What a statement! If He had to learn obedience, we should not be surprised that we do as well! We are told that Jesus was obedient, even to the point of death – death on a cross.

Praise for Obedience

Because of Jesus' obedience, scripture says God glorified Him. We need to heap praise on our children when they are obedient. Talk to them about how it feels good to obey, about how it makes Mom and Dad happy. When they disobey, it makes the parent sad, the child's heart feels troubled and they feel yucky inside.

Intentional Parenting

If YOU were a Rebel

What if you were a rebel? You may feel unqualified to deal with your child's rebellion. But if you don't do it, who will? If you still have stuff to work through in your own life, see a counselor, or work through "Deconstructing Rebellion" from the *Freedom Resource Manual*. You can repent, change and be an example to your child. Don't let your past stop you from building your child's future.

How can parents set a good example for their children regarding rebellion? Don't laugh when they are naughty. (You may have to turn your back or go to another room.) It won't be cute when they are 15 and bigger than you! Don't complain about those in authority in front of your child. Don't break traffic laws. Don't tell stories glorifying your past rebellion. If you came to faith later in life, take time to explain to your children what has happened, why you have changed. Apologize for your past mistakes. Teach and explain the new standard and the moral reasons for your decisions. Take time to make sure they understand. Then be consistent in enforcing them. Give them time to come to faith themselves without pushing them. Discuss changes in your home, such as movies they can no longer

Intentional Parenting

watch. Be loving and patient. God was patient all those years with you.

Identifying Rebellion

Some kinds of rebellion are obvious. Junior stomps his foot and says, "NO!" Other overt kinds of rebellion might be throwing a temper tantrum, or crying to make you miserable and change your mind. With older kids, they may roll their eyes or give you a disgusted "look".

Here are some more subtle forms of rebellion that are less easily noticed, yet they are rebellion all the same.
- Arguing, even politely
- Whining, complaining to get out of obeying
- Crying to make you change your mind
- Making excuses not to obey ("I can't…" or "It's too hard…"
- Feeling they are exempted from obedience for some reason – special circumstances so they don't have to obey.
- Selective listening
- Delayed obedience or obeying in their own way.
- Partial obedience. (Picking up toys – but throwing them.)

- Obeying with a bad attitude or while making faces
- Staying in control (Finding ways to get around authority, rules)
- Giving up rather than obeying ("I just can't do it.")

You MUST deal with these things – do not skip over this. Correct the HEART, not just the actions! Remember this is not about making you feel good because your children mind, it is for their good.

Quickly and Quietly

We borrowed a phrase from Susannah Wesley who raised 16 children including the great men of faith, Charles and John Wesley. Some of the time she raised her children without the help of her husband (who separated from her for a season over a political disagreement). The children were to "obey quickly and quietly." There could not be screaming and crying in protest. Again, remember, they are saying, "Not your will, but MINE be done," if they argue and disobey. We also required the corrected child to, "Cry quietly."

The Strong-Willed Child

What about the proverbial strong-willed child? The first parenting book I ever read was Dr. James Dobson's book by that name. I was desperate, because my first born was so strong-willed. I was often in tears trying to get him to obey. It was a constant and wearing battle. Looking back, he was probably stronger than I was. But I couldn't let him win. He would lose in life. My husband and I worked very hard to train him, and today he is a wonderful person, a terrific dad, and a joy to us both.

Dr. Dobson's emphasis is that the child is testing the validity and the strength of your authority. Are you worth following? You must be consistent with your standards and your requirements. Do not allow mixed messages (what's okay today isn't tomorrow…). Keep your word even if it hurts to do so. A friend of ours with a strong-willed 3-year old daughter was asked how they managed to keep going with the battle. He replied, "I never let her win." She turned out great!

It is possible to find yourself constantly set against a child, constantly battling them, and lose your enjoyment of their childhood. Don't let that happen. Remember that God gave this child this personality. It is a part of the destiny God has for them. They will probably need all this strength for what they will go through as an adult or in order to fulfill the calling God has for them. It's up to you to shape it in the early years to prepare them for that.

Is Teenage Rebellion to be Expected?
Some voices in our culture say that it is normal to rebel as a teenager. I don't accept that. I maintain that life is one long path in the same direction. Your child's behavior, personality, and character are a process. You can guard that process. Watch over the thousands of decisions and heart-choices that lead to your child's teen years. (See Chapter 19.)

Beware of disagreements or misunderstandings with your child that devalue them or their experiences. One of our children had a powerful experience at youth camp. Although she had accepted Jesus at a young age, she insisted that this was really her conversion. Her dad and I argued with her and tried to explain. We were a little hurt by what seemed like an invalidation of our prior experience with her. We hurt her feelings by not accepting her experience. It actually became something that the enemy used to tell her we didn't believe her or understand her.

What about PK's and MK's?

Pastor's Kids (or MK's – Missionaries' Kids) are often expected to rebel and throw off the restrictions they have grown up with. Again I must say, keep encouraging obedience along that long path. Do not allow members of the congregation to put extra expectations on your kids. Let them be normal. Whatever is good enough behavior for your family (without ministry pressures) and whatever is good enough for them to stand before God with, whether clothing or music or language, is good enough for *anyone*. Protect them from well-meaning people who try to put pressure on them to perform for the sake of appearance because of your ministry.

Keep Talking

It is tempting to pull back from a child who is rebelling against the family. Keep communicating, keep expressing your love. Don't be the one who allows isolation and alienation to multiply the injuries of rebellion.

Endnotes

1 Samuel 15:22-23
Jeremiah 4:16-18

Intentional Parenting

Hebrews 5:8
Luke 22:42; Philippians 2:8
Philippians 2:8-11
Freedom Resource Manual – free online download
The New Strong-Willed Child by Dr. James Dobson
Psalm 15:4

Chapter 16
Quick Reference to Specific Behavior Problems

Part of being an Intentional Parent is addressing character issues and misbehavior with the truths of scripture, and training your children to align their lives with God's word. The rewards are definitely worth the hard work. This chapter is contains an alphabetized list of possible issues.

Christians are called to live at a higher level than the average family in our culture. Life is not just about being a good person. Our lives are rooted in becoming more and more like Jesus. Our highest purpose is found in wanting to please God. While salvation is a free gift, paid for by Jesus' death, burial and resurrections, we know we will be judged and rewarded according to what we do in this life.

Without such spiritual motivation, what do worldly people live for? Pleasing themselves? Looking good? Making their life on earth as heaven-like as possible? Having a family they can be proud of? Demonstrating that they have everything together? These seem to fall far short of the higher road of the Christian life. Disappointments and failings would be even more devastating if everything only depended on you and was only for the here and now.

Intentional Parenting

Because most parents begin with parenting by dealing with what they *don't* like in their child's behavior, this list is categorized by the negative behavior to put off rather than the positive actions to put on. You may want to refer to the traits lists with opposites on pages 112-114 for the positives. Unfortunately, because of the sin nature, these negative things seem to come more naturally than the opposite positive behavior.

Aggression, bullying

Humanism says this is part of the idea of 'survival of the fittest', but we are not animals. This one-upmanship may be rooted in pride, fulfilling a desire to put others down and to be the one to rule over others. Have the offender do nice things for the victim. Have them say complementary things instead of name calling. Teach them to be others-minded.

Aggressions may also be an attempt to compete for love and affection given do to accomplishment. Check to make sure you are treating all kids the same.

Anger

See chapter 8

Intentional Parenting

Arguing

Do your children argue with you when you ask them to do something? You should not allow it. Remember, what you allow is being trained into them. It is judicious to consider new information the child might want to present (if you don't have the whole picture), but if it is a matter of they think they know best or just plain don't want to do what they are told, stop the arguing quickly. For young children or children who habitually argue with you, make them obey before you explain anything. For older kids, they should know the reason why or you should take time to explain it. Remember, the goal is understanding what to do in grown-up life, not blind obedience.

Behavior in Public

I remember growing up hearing, "Children are to be seen and not heard." I don't agree with it as a practice, but when you are around kids who misbehave in public, you may find yourself wishing for a little more of those old ways.

There are several things you can do to make sure your kids behave well in public.
1. Explain in advance to the child where you are going, what it is like there, and how you want them to act

while you are there. You can set them up for success by explaining. For example, "We are going to the library. You must be quiet there. We use very soft voices in this place so people are not disturbed while reading. That is the rule for everyone, including grown-ups. You need to stay by me and not wander off or run around. You may check out as many books as you can carry. When I say it is time to go, we will leave with no fussing or whining, okay?"

Grocery store: "We are going to the grocery store. I have a very specific list of what we need. You may not whine and beg for things. I do not have money today for extra treats. You may not put things in the cart when I am not looking. You must stay right beside me and not wander off. If you do not obey, I will take you to the car and spank you. Do you understand?"

At the park: "We are going to the park. It is breezy today, so you need a sweater. You may not take off your sweater or shoes without my permission. You cannot go away from the playground without me. Do not throw the sand around. I don't want it in your hair. There will be strangers there, but I will not leave you, and you are not to go with anyone else. Please, be polite to people and say, 'Hello.' You can (or cannot) play on the big rocks. We will all leave together when it is time to come home."

At a wedding: "We are going to John and Tina's wedding today. They are getting married and beginning their own home and family. This is a very special day for them. We will be very quiet while we watch the ceremony. If you have a question, you must whisper it to me. If you need to go to the bathroom, you must whisper and tell me. I want you to stay by me and not run around, even during the party afterward. If you want to go talk to a friend, I need to come with you."

At church: "We are going to church. I want you to be respectful because this is a special place. Do not run around in the building. Listen quietly when the pastor or someone on the stage is speaking. I want you to stand when everyone stands and sit when

Intentional Parenting

everyone sits. I want you to sing with the congregation if you can. If you are tired, remember that Jesus was tired when He died on the cross for you. You must still participate."

2. Now you must enforce your plan. Do not weaken and yield to whining or all out tantrums. Kids know when they've got you over a barrel and you'll give them anything to stop the embarrassment you feel. Be willing to pick them up, apologize to those around you and take them home early if necessary. Say, "I'm sorry for Johnny's behavior. We are working on this. Excuse me. We've got to go."

Behavior with Company

Teach your child how to be a good guest. If you are visiting someone for the first time, they should ask permission before going to another room to play or wait to be invited. Find out what the boundaries are in this home. Where are children allowed to be? What bathroom should they use?

If your child spills something, you should clean it up, getting them to help if they are old enough. If your child damages something, you should replace it and help your child with earning money to pay for it. (Don't let this slide if the hostess says not to worry about it. It is important to your child's training.)

When it is time to go, give your child a warning a few minutes before you want to go. Have them pick up toys, then say their good-byes. You would not want to have to leave abruptly, and it isn't pleasant for them. Yet, they should obey you when it is time to go. This also means you must not keep on talking and talking, negating the time frame you have stated.

Cheating, Stealing

Cheating is stealing answers or the work of someone else. Explain to your child that a teacher needs to see what they know. It isn't about short term approval. Learning is a process.

Stealing is based in selfishness. Talk to your child about the feelings of the other person, about their loss. Make them return the item and make restitution. Several of my children have memories of going back to the grocery store to return gum or candy. I made them pay for things and apologize to the store manager.

Contrariness

See page 118 on Contrarians

Control

While the scripture admonishes us to be self-controlled, that is not the same as being controlling. Some people try hard to control others and circumstances. Some personality types have a need to feel like they are in control of their world and the decisions that affect them. You may find yourself in repeated power struggles with a child with a strong personality. Yet, in this life there is so much we cannot control. Training your child to understand that their control is limited does them the favor of preparing them for life.

Try to set a good balance for your child by allowing them control in some small ways. Perhaps they have chores to do. You can allow them to control when they do them. If you want them done early in the day you can offer a reward if they are done by a certain time, but no reward if they are done later. They still have to be done. Consequences apply if they are not finished.

As the child gets older and shows more responsibility, release more and more things to his or her control and responsibility. Young children have a smaller "control allowance".

Cursing, bad language

Vulgarity and cursing are so much a part of our culture, that people often accept stronger and stronger language as normal. Jesus said that our yes should simply be yes and our no just a plain no. Anything more is a trap. The apostle Paul said our language should be wholesome and uplifting to others. I believe the coarseness that has arisen in our society is in direct proportion to the loss of the ideals of femininity. The strong mother and the firm teacher who shake their finger at a young generation, telling them to watch their manners and their language, have become passé. That's too bad. So many other areas have become viler, more violent, and more vulgar. Don't be afraid to draw the line at bad language and cursing.

You may need to teach your kids appropriate expressions for their frustration. Words like, "Rats!" or "Phooey!" may be useful. "Drat" works for a lot of things. Set a high standard and stick to it.

Cruelty

The world laughs at baseness and evil. Hit movies tout meanness, nasty behavior, and snide words. Sinful people have been calling good evil and evil good for centuries. The earth was filled with violence at the time of Noah's flood. Don't let this kind of anger and viciousness have a place in your home. I've seen parents laugh at a child being cruel to an animal. Unbelievable! What do they think the child will be doing when they are an adult? Committing assault or murder!? Don't set them up!

Disrespect

See chapter 12.

Discontent, dissatisfaction, complaining

There is no standard amount of money or possessions everyone deserves or gets. Billions of people in the world live on what Americans would consider a miniscule amount of money every month. Having the latest version of popular electronic gadgets or getting pampering spa treatments is not a necessity. It is the job of advertisers to make us want more and more things. Americans often get wrapped up in consumerism.

Intentional Parenting

As adults, we can make sure we are not speaking discontented, unthankful words about our possessions and way of life. The nation of Israel was known for complaining all through the exodus from Egypt.

For children, we must teach them to be thankful for and content with what they have. It's all right to look forward to something new, say for a birthday. It's very good to teach kids to earn money and save up for larger purchases and extra activities. If there is work behind possession, we all value the item more. You can tell your children about what you are saving up for or let them go with you when you purchase that long-awaited item. (Obviously, don't demonstrate using a credit card to avoid the waiting.)

You can provide opportunities to do extra chores (not the everyday variety) to earn money so they can buy that gadget. Do not overpay for chores. If chores are worth $1 each, do not pay $5 so they can get what they want. Let this kind of activity be a life lesson.

We had a ticket system when the kids were little. They could earn tickets (sold in big rolls in educational toy stores) and use them to buy goodies from a treasure chest or extra privileges like renting a movie they wanted to see. I bought items from the dollar store or discount store, then

Intentional Parenting

priced them by the value of the tickets. A $1 item might cost 20 tickets. Think about how many tickets your kids can earn in a week, then convert that into what you can afford that to be worth. If your kids can earn 100 tickets per week, you probably can't afford for those to be worth $1 each.

If a child carelessly breaks a toy, do not replace it right away. Your compassionate heart may want to do so, but that is not helpful over the long term. Real life has consequences. If we do not take care of our possessions as adults, we suffer dire consequences. It is cheaper to learn this young, that still be trying to figure it out at 25 or 30.

It is good that young adults (and children) understand the value of money. If a child wants a $20 video game, let them do 20 chores to earn the money to buy it. Teach them to watch for it to go on sale. Teenagers may want a new sports car, but a cheap old car costing $5000 is the equivalent of 700 hours of work at minimum wage. That is 28 weeks of full-time work with no money taken out for taxes! A part-timer would work a whole year, just for a car. Then there would be repairs, gas, and insurance. If they get a ticket for speeding, the costs will go up. If you give everything to your child, you rob them of a valuable lesson. We had several teens at once, so we had an older (code: "beater") vehicle we let them drive. As parents we took care of the plates and maintenance, but the kids had to buy their own gas and insurance. Even with that, they found it was not worth it to drive before age 18. If they worked part-time, the expense of driving took a lot of their money. (Welcome to the world of grown-ups!)

All this said, gifts are for giving. We tried to give both useful and practical gifts for birthdays and Christmas. We might give something that could be used with something they had bought or earned, but we did not try to substitute or come up with what they were working for themselves. If they were saving up for something large, we might give them money to add to their savings for that item.

Fearfulness

I find that many parents are just plain fearful. They are afraid the child will be in an accident. They are afraid they will not do well in school. They are afraid to travel. They are afraid to miss the experience of traveling. On and on it goes. Their lives are ruled by fear.

To start with, you as an adult must conquer this. I don't believe it is possible to raise our children to be something we are not. Tackle your fears and worries. The

Bible commands us to do so when it says, "Be anxious for nothing…" After that, we must help our children be confident that they can handle whatever situations arise, that they are liked by other people, that they have the capacity to be pleasant no matter what. We can also help them feel secure and well-cared for by making sure their everyday needs are met at a comfortable level. (See Appendix 3 for my clothing list.)

Secondly, do not start your communication with fear. When you explain why a child should or should not do something, let it be about moral reasoning, not your fears.

Let your child know that if a problem comes up, whether it is a broken shoe or a bully at school, you are there to help them and care for them. You will go to bat for them. You will not leave them to figure things out on their own. If they are teens, you will discuss ways to deal with the problem and you will be their back-up.

Build confidence and faith towards God into your children and into yourself.

Fighting

See aggression, bullying, anger, sibling rivalry, wrestling in this chapter.

Intentional Parenting

Focus, Lack of

The numbers of children diagnosed in our schools with dyslexia and attention deficit disorder is astounding and disturbing. While your children are small, there are things you can do to help prevent this. Make sure they crawl before they walk. The motion of crawling requires balance as a child moves a right hand with a left knee. This seems to create more connections between the two hemispheres of the brain, something lacking in children with dyslexia.

Help young children focus and concentrate for periods of 10 minutes or so. Make them sit still through dinner and not keep getting up and down. Have them color or draw for 10 minutes or so without jumping to other activities. Help them finish activities and then put toys away before starting something else. Do not allow the majority of their time to be spent with television programs that change activities every couple of minutes. I believe we have generations of adults who cannot sit still longer than the 8 minutes between commercial breaks. Read chapter books to your elementary-age children, sitting quietly and listening for 20-30 minutes each day.

If your child has dyslexia, have them do balancing exercises before they try to do schoolwork or homework.

The "fencer's lunge" or walking on a low balance beam is helpful. We built one in our backyard by putting each of the ends of a 4 X 4 post into a cinderblock. Lay out a jump rope in a zigzag or figure-eight pattern and have the child walk on it. Another helpful resource is **www.DianneCraft.org**. She is a special needs teacher in Denver with training for parents. Her brain gym exercises really help kids with learning disabilities.

Forgetfulness

Help your child think in an orderly way. You may need reminders like chore charts or perhaps to train them to set out their clothes and backpacks for the next day rather than rushing and then forgetting when they are in a time crunch.

Help older children use homework folders and planner calendars to create good time management habits in their formative years. You may want to keep a family calendar with different boxes for each member, but teach kids to keep their own calendar as well when they are older. I think it is helpful to do a three-week look-ahead each Friday. That way you have time to plan for special events, find out if you need to provide snacks for a group, and keep your finger on the pulse of how busy your life is. You then have enough lead time to know whether that schedule is too hectic or just about right.

Even Einstein did not try to keep small bits of information in his head. He said it was available to be looked up.

Friends – Bad
Somehow there are seldom questions about friendships other than ones that are a negative influence. Scripture says, "Bad company corrupts good character." The good child does not rub off on the bad one and improve him or her. It's always the other way around.

Even during the teen years you have the right *and* the responsibility to filter the flow of who you allow in your home and how often. Don't be afraid to exercise your power here. I've never regretted being too careful, only not being careful enough. Sometimes certain friends are not a healthy influence. You may need to cut off contact with that person or family. I pray for God's help for them, but it will have to come from somewhere other than my child.

Do not allow friends of the opposite sex to be alone with your teen in your home. The bad possibilities are large and many. Kids learn things from other kids that you would never want them exposed to. It may be inconvenient, but you need to chaperone everything. Teens and young adults who are sexually active often started while home without supervision.

When it comes to your child visiting the homes of others, make sure you have been in the home and know the people well.

Gambling

I wanted to teach my kids about the foolishness of gambling. When they were early teens, I set up a game of bingo, with each kid getting 100 dried beans or so. They had to ante up 10 beans for a game. We played enough games for them to lose most of their beans to one sibling. (That child saw the lesson of the others even though they won.) I explained how this worked with money and explained the odds of winning most popular games of chance (VERY slim). Lesson learned.

Gossip

Of all the areas where grown-ups fail to set good examples for kids, this is likely the most common. Scriptures abound about gossip. It is a damaging and dangerous vice. Again, you cannot take your child where you are not willing to go. Here are some questions to ask yourself when you wonder: Is it gossip?

- Does the person I am speaking with need to know about this? If yes, am I the right person to tell them?
- Would I say this if the person about whom I am talking were present?
- If this is something I need to iron out with another person, go to them. Don't talk to others about it. (Exception – you should talk to your spouse or a mentor who will help you sort out your feelings and who will encourage you to take steps to work things through.)
- Why do I want to tell others about this? What is my motivation? Am I seeking sympathy? Is negativity a thrill to me? Can this person do anything about the situation? If it is just loose talk, stop immediately. If it is one-upmanship or sharing negativity, stop.
- Is this conversation edifying? Will the person feel like they've been thrown-up on after what I have to say?

Intentional Parenting

If you can train this kind of thinking and behavior into your child, what an advantage for life! They will have fewer quarrels, less strife and less to clean up in relationships.

Gratefulness (Lack of)* or *Entitlement

Lack of gratitude is a dangerous thing. One cannot allow children to think that everything should be given to them. I think we had an advantage in not being able to afford to give our children each new toy or gadget that came out. By earning and saving to obtain those things, our children were much more thankful.

Sometimes parents who are away from home too much, or those who are divorced try to compensate by giving their child "stuff" instead. If you are giving your children everything they want and they do not think they should have to work hard, pull back and help them earn more. Teach them to have a good work ethic and value what they have.

Romans 1 talks about the sad condition of those who were not thankful to God. They took much in life for granted, worshiped the creature rather than the Creator, and were engrossed in homosexuality.

Intentional Parenting

Greed / Covetousness

Greed is an intense desire for something, such as possessions, food or power. It leads to a willingness to circumvent morality in order to gain those things. As a parent you must moderate your child's desires. You must instruct them in ways that allow for goals, but not greediness. Covetousness is desiring those things than belong to others. The covetous person may envy the person who possesses them. They wish that they owned the possessions instead.

Unfortunately, these traits are easily birthed in the sinful nature of humankind. They are one of the destructive things that we parents much weed out of our children's lives. As with natural gardening, it is much easier to catch these things while they are small than to pull up tree-sized problems. Be attentive and speak to situations. Teach your children to be glad for others when they succeed or when they obtain new possessions.

Grumpiness

(See also *Whining*) Scripture says, "A merry heart does good like a medicine…" We are to "rejoice in the Lord always…" Joy is one of the fruits of the Spirit. Whether someone is a morning person or a night owl, they have to be able to meet each day with a positive outlook. Good things happen to those who are looking for them.

For pre-teen girls who are beginning to learn about the emotions connected to hormone changes (PMS), they need to know they will deal with this stuff for many years. They do not want a life that explodes and is nasty and rude every month. They don't want to be known for this. Teach them to control their words, even if their feelings are all over the map. Moms have a day here and there where they must pray more and bite their tongues until they feel better.

Harshness

See "kind words only" practice on pages 86-87.

Hate

Hate is an ungodly emotion. It is the opposite of love, God's character. John said we cannot hate our brother (or friend) and claim to be a believer. The two simply do not go together. You cannot mix light and darkness. As for saying, "I hate you!" I would not allow such talk. It is hurtful and evil. The scriptures on bad language also apply to this.

Often hate is rooted in selfishness. When one does not get what they want, they may resent it and allow that to breed hatred.

The life of the Christian is one of constant contradiction with the ways of the world. Jesus always required those who followed Him to live by a higher standard. This is certainly true when people are mean or unjust toward us. We must be forgiving (though perhaps not trusting) and kind, though the offender may not deserve it.

Interrupting

Many parents think nothing of children interrupting adult conversation. I believe this is evidence of child-centeredness. What the child wants is not the most important thing in the moment, though he or she may think it is. Teach your child to be considerate, not rude. Have them stand by you quietly and wait for a pause in the conversation. Then they can ask their question. You might teach them to put their hand on your arm to let you know they need something and then wait until you pause to see about them. This is a bit of a lesson in self-control as well. Make sure that you don't make them wait too long, or you will defeat the purpose of this training.

Children are notorious for interrupting (especially for tattling) when you are on the phone. Even small children sense that you are not tuned in to what they are doing. They may even think you can't pay attention to more than one thing at a time. Be willing to excuse yourself from the conversation and deal with misbehavior. Call your friend back if necessary. The worst thing you can do is ignore bad behavior.

If children interrupt each other during a conversation, try an egg-timer (3 minutes). They can watch the salt sift down and not be allowed to speak until after the time is up.

Irresponsibility

How many adults in this life have difficulty with being responsible? Their problems are always someone else's fault. Their marriages would be great if their spouse would just get it together. Their jobs would be happy if their bosses were not such jerks. They would be successful if not for someone else who got in the way.

We certainly want to raise our children to do better than this. Start out with small responsibilities, like picking up toys. Work up to bigger responsibilities like doing their own laundry or picking a sibling up after school. As kids show responsibility in the lower level duties, give them a bit larger duties. And with the greater responsibility, give them a bit more freedom. A child who does his own laundry well could perhaps pick out his own clothes when you go shopping.

This also means that a child who does not take care of their responsibilities must have consequences. Once when our youngest child had to do the "pooper scooper" chore (which rotated amongst the kids from week to week), we found that there was way more poo to clean up than a week's-worth. That meant that the previous week, the chore had not been done. I called together the kid whose chore it had been and ordered them to pay the youngest child for doing what they had left undone. This was a two-fold lesson. People who don't want to do their chores *can* pay someone else to do them. Yet being sure it was done was still their responsibility. Also, they learned that it was hurtful to the other person who felt taken advantage of.

What about a child who does not take care of her possessions? If she is careless or rough with items, causing them to break, the parent should not replace them. Help the child learn to value things by having to work to earn money to buy them.

Jealousy, Envy

Scripture says jealousy is as cruel as the grave. While this is especially true in marriage, it can become so in sibling relationships as well. Teach your kids to root for each other, to be excited for the success of their friends, and to appreciate the attractive qualities in their siblings.

Jealousy of looks: Thinking negatively about themselves, wishing they looked like someone else is most especially destructive. Wanting to be taller if they are short, wanting to be curvier if they are straight, and so on only sets themselves up for a lifetime of dissatisfaction. These things are what they are. The rise of anorexia and bulimia in pre-teens and teens is appalling. I am shocked at the teenagers who are getting plastic surgery! Read Is. 45:9. Teach them to embrace the way God has made them. Discuss the sadness of the movie star who is always getting yet another surgery to look young. Your children will be living with how they are made for a lifetime. Love it! Be thankful for your health and strength. Be positive about the Creator's design.

Jealousy of talents: Being envious of others gifts and talents is just plain unproductive. I might wish I'd been gifted to be a prodigy in music, but wasting thought on it, pining for musical accomplishments or being jealous of the person with an outstanding voice is totally futile. God decides what He chooses to place within us. That's it. We can make the most of what we have; we can practice and take lessons and be disciplined. In that way we can surpass the accomplishments of the genius who is lazy. But it won't put us on par with the naturally gifted person who works hard. We must each find what we are good at and explore those possibilities.

Jealousy of friends or popularity: Some people make friends more easily than others. They have outgoing personalities. Perhaps they have life experience that has put them more at ease. Teach your children how to be friendly, how to make small talk (see Chapter 17), and how to be a good friend. They will have all the friends they need. Popularity is a fleeting thing. It can come and go as you can see from the covers of magazines. Frequently a popular person is happy-go-lucky and fun to be around. Some of that can be developed. Sometimes they are also irresponsible in deeper ways.

One of the most important skills you can impart to your child is how to embrace God's design in how they are made and what they have. The way they look, their level of intelligence, the things they are good at, and so on, were made to fulfill the destiny God has for them in the kingdom. Contentedness if a gift. And it is a requirement in the kingdom.

Judgmental

Have you ever known someone with a critical spirit? Nothing is ever good enough? This is not the same thing as coaching someone to excellence, mixing correction with affirmation. It is not the same thing as looking for fruit in the lives of those who claim to be believers. It is a nastiness that judges the value of others to be less, always less. It is harsh in word and in deed, constantly evaluating others and finding they don't measure up.

This person may be overly pleased with themselves, or they may be just as hard on themselves. Either way, they are difficult to live with and their children grow up scarred and dysfunctional. They do not think they can succeed, because nothing will be good enough.

Do not allow children to be this way, and do not impose this on your family. If you are a perfectionist, learn to accept "good enough". If you are judgmental, learn to leave that business to God.

Laziness

A part of human nature wants things to go easily, but it is a result of Adam's fall that our work often fights against us or is just plain difficult.

Teach your kids that what they have will largely be as a result of their investment of labor. There are many verses in Proverbs about poverty coming to the lazy person. If a child is prone to laziness, teach them to do things correctly the first time so they don't have to redo it. I used to tell my kids that if they were lazy, it must mean they needed more practice. I would have them do the chore for another week rather than pass it on to the next kid in the rotation the next week. Or I would give them extra work to teach them to enjoy work, or at least not to avoid what is necessary.

Lying

Lying is condemned in scripture, yet it is a common failing in our culture. People lie in order to look better or to get what they want. Parents are often dismayed when young children lie, amazed that this particular sin has already begun. You must deal firmly with lying. You do not want to allow kids to become "good at this." At first you will be easily able to tell they are lying. Eventually, maybe not. We gave extra swats for lying. We might say, you will get 2 swats if you did such and such, but if you lie to me, I will give you 4 swats.

If you are not sure where the truth starts and stops, pray. Ask the Lord to give you ideas of questions to ask, evidence to look for. Do your best. Then give out strong discipline for lying.

Messiness

One of the components of responsibility is taking care of our possessions. Some people are naturally "neat freaks" while others are not. When God placed Adam and Eve in the Garden at the beginning of time, He gave them dominion and told them they were to rule it, subdue it and make it fruitful. We each have possessions and spaces over which we have dominion. Keeping them clean and orderly is part of dominion and stewardship over responsibilities.

There is a difference between clutter and dirt. Do not allow dirty conditions to remain anywhere in your home. Stains and spills contain germs and are breeding grounds for bacteria. Regular, thorough cleaning is a must. When little ones are being potty trained, I found I had to wipe down the toilet and surrounding area every day in order to be sanitary. When the kids were young and we were all at home most of

Intentional Parenting

the time, the dishwasher had to run twice a day to keep up. This was a matter of doing whatever it took to be healthy and peaceful. Realistically, this is keeping a clean house is quite a bit of work when kids are too young to help. (See Chapter 17 for when they can learn.) It will require teamwork and patience by parents to keep things clean.

With regard to clutter, I did not mind kids making a mess, but it always had to be cleaned up. For general purposes we had a "toy break" to clean up before lunch (we read then had naps after lunch) and again after dinner before bed. If someone was working on a project, we discussed the length of time their things could be out and when the project was to be finished. Also, I allowed toys in the family room, but not in the living room. That way if company dropped by, there was a room in which grow-ups could visit without the kid clutter. My goal was a peaceful and inviting home.

If kids' rooms are too messy, consider whether they have too many toys, too much stuff. Or perhaps they do not have enough storage space. Our daughter sorts toys into a number of plastic bins, and puts some in the garage. Every few months she switches out the bins. The kids respond like they've gotten new toys. They enjoy things more and there is less to pick up.

Train your kids to a high standard. When they leave home they will live up to it. Their future spouses will thank you.

Passivity

Some wives equate submission in marriage as synonymous with passivity. A better demonstration of submission is to aggressively support one's spouse and to make teamwork and partnership a priority. This is more proactive and positive.

A child may become passive in response to others being overbearing. Teach children to express their opinions (albeit, respectfully) and their desires. Respond with reasonable direction (not the same as self-doubt). Do not allow the dominant sibling to always have their way. Do not allow a child to always go along to get along. Even the child who wants everyone to be happy and get along must have an opinion from time to time and be encouraged to express it.

People (children included) cannot stuff their feelings forever. Someone who is going along to get along is likely to explode at some point. You cannot suppress emotions indefinitely. The bottled up pressure must eventually be released. Passive-aggressive behavior is exhibited in going along on the outside, but rebelling or getting even in sly ways.

Having an open communication, saying what needs to be said, keeping the air cleared will prevent this unhealthy process.

People-pleasing / Fear of Man

Some personalities need approval more than others. Some young people are fine with disagreeing with the trends or others opinions. Some are not. This can become a dangerous effort in people-pleasing and eventually an approval addiction. It can especially lead to verbal and emotional abuse, possibly by those in authority.

Teach your children to be honest with their opinions and thoughts. They should not go along or agree in order to gain approval or prevent disagreements. They should especially not be willing to go along with lies, deception or manipulation by others. They need to respect conflict as productive, not avoid it. One man said as a youth he never offered an opinion on where to go out to eat, even when asked. He was more concerned that others be happy and approving. Scripture calls it "fear of man" meaning being more interested an approval from people than approval from God. This is dangerous to a person's self-worth and sets them up for secretive destructive behavior. Teach your children that honest communication is refreshing to all.

Pessimism, Negativity

The proverbial glass-half-empty/glass-half-full conundrum can plague your parenting. Guard against negativity. Sure you have a lot of work to do with your children, but it will not always be so. Train your children to be more positive than negative. Rate yourself once a month on how you are doing on a scale of 1 to 10 (with 10 being most positive) to evaluate how you are doing with this. Years ago, my husband and I needed to work on negativity and complaining. We had a jar with a slot in the top. Every time one of us was negative, we had to put a quarter in the "negative jar". Each of us had permission to "ahem" the other to put a quarter in the jar. It made us much more aware of what we were saying and bad habits we had gotten into. When our kids were growing up, we used nickels for a while to train them similarly. We gave each child 20 nickels at the beginning of the week and collect a nickel for each negative statement. If they had nickels left at the end of the week they could spend them.

Intentional Parenting

Picky Eaters - Bad Eating Habits

This is the subject that seems to come up when I am in the company of a group of grandparents or great-grandparents. When I mention that I am writing a book on parenting, they frequently bring up picky eaters. The older generation (some of whom lived through the Great Depression or the lean times after World War II) is disgusted with the tendency in the young generation to only eat the few foods that they especially like. If your child will only eat mac and cheese or peanut butter and jelly, it's time to pull yourself together and train your child to eat a variety of foods. You never know where life may take you. You may end up living in a foreign country without the conveniences and choices you prefer. Hard times may come to our nation, and what is available may change. You may find your finances don't allow you to purchase the prepared food items they want. And most important of all, you want your kids to be healthy, so that includes eating fruits and vegetables and a variety of things.

    Here are some tips for what to train into your picky eaters:

1. Preferences do not equal requirements. You only have to chew and swallow. You do not have to enjoy. Basic nutrition is the priority.

2. You must take one or two bites of everything. This helps develop a taste for variety. When small, my children did not like strawberries. (Crazy, huh?!) Or asparagus. Over time, a few bites here and a few bites there, they learned to like both.
3. If you do not want to eat what is being served, you may eat your one or two bites, but that is all you get for tonight. Mom is not a short-order cook. She will not make you something else. There will be no substitutes (like PBJ) and no dessert. There will be no popcorn with the movie we are watching together later. If kids choose to go to bed hungry, they will not starve by morning.
4. Don't use food as the only reward or fun activity. Pizza or ice cream are okay for an occasional treat or reward, but if all your incentives are food, you are sending a message that equates success with eating. This is all too common for people who struggle with weight issues. Have other kinds of rewards: stickers, bookmarks, toys, etc.

Remember again – what does this behavior look like in five years? As an adult? Are you setting them up for weight problems? Are you raising a picky spouse who will not be easy to please no matter whom they marry? Will they teach their children to eat healthy? Like everything else in parenting, we must do what is good for them, not only because it makes our life easier, but it makes their future brighter. Embrace the hard work!

Pride, Boasting

It is good to have an honest opinion of oneself. That includes a clear view of both strengths *and* weakness. A person who sees those strengths and abilities in an exaggerated way, minimizing their weaknesses and faults, can be full of pride, one of the seven deadly sins. First of all, we can only be grateful for how God made us. We could have been born with handicaps or in a mud hut in a third-world country. Scripture says we are to have an honest opinion of ourselves and to be concerned for the interest of *others* more than our own.

It is good to celebrate our moments of accomplishment, but we are also to be happy for others' success. After that, we should not go around with an "I am SO good!" attitude. I believe real self-worth comes from making real accomplishments. Yet scripture says if we boast about anything, let it be a boast that we know the Lord.

So if your child drifts into this area of pride, correct it. Do not let it grow. Scripture says pride goes before a fall. It also says that God resists the proud. That means He will fight against the success of a proud person. And it says God will not share his glory (the praise He is due) with anyone. Don't let this become a life-dominating pattern in your child. Train a balanced attitude into them of appreciating how God has made them and helped them. Help them acknowledge the gifts in others. Teach them to celebrate successes, but not to live there in their minds, defined by that event.

Be aware of your child's heart. Even good behavior can be undergirded with wrong motives. One child did her own chores for the sake of pride – that she was better because she did hers. Yet she was unwilling to help others with their chores or participate in teamwork projects with the family. It would be easy to approve and affirm that she did her chores, yet miss the more important issue of the heart.

Pouting / The Silent Treatment
Some families use the silent treatment as a means of retaliation. If you don't get your way, you punish others by

not talking to them. For some it is a passive-aggressive means of rebellion. Often I think of the second half of the verse in Proverbs about spanking; "Do not let your soul despair for their crying." Or their pouting. Stick to your guns, and don't give into this kind of manipulation. If your family of origin acted this way, check your heart to see if it trained fear of man or people-pleasing into you.

Procrastination

Procrastination is such a time-thief. Usually it takes more time and energy to put things off and put things off than to just do them. Perfectionists tend to put things off, thinking they will be able to do them more perfectly if they delay until they have more time to give to the project. Teach your child to get things done and out of the way. Help them see that when chores are out of the way, they have free time. My kids learned that if they got their homeschooling work done by 2 PM, they had lots of time to play and do fun activities. It was their choice. They could drag it out until 5 or they could get it finished. This also helped with their work ethic. They know how to work with intensity when it is time to work, and to fully relax and enjoy free time when that time comes.

Intentional Parenting

Punctuality, lack of

Being late for everything puts you at a disadvantage. Teach your child to manage time well in preparing to go somewhere. Set a timer on the stove for 10 minutes before time to leave. That warning means brush your teeth, grab your shoes and coat, get your stuff. We go out the door (reset the timer) in exactly 10 minutes – whether you are still in your pajamas or not.

Be realistic in assessing how long it takes to get somewhere, including any extra stops on the way. A friend who was always late used to plan an extra errand stop on the way. She never allowed extra time, but used that as an excuse for her tardiness.

One year when we were attending Christian school, I told the kids that if they could not be ready on time to leave, I could get them up 15 minutes earlier the next day. (I knew that they did have enough time, but just weren't using it well.) If that didn't work I would get them up 15 minutes earlier than *that* the following day. It was their choice to manage and be ready or I would make the adjustments and consequences to force improvement. I think I only had to do it once. Of course, don't threaten anything on which that you are not absolutely committed to follow through.

Intentional Parenting

Even if you are going to dinner at a friend's house, your punctuality communicates that you value them and their time. By being on time, you are teaching your child to manage their time and to be considerate of others.

RAD – Reactive Attachment Disorder

Sometimes adopted or foster children have extreme challenges due to past abuse or neglect. This may require professional assistance or therapy. My husband has found TCU Institute of Child Development to be a good resource. (www.child.tcu.edu) Here is a quote from their website:

> *The TCU Institute of Child Development strives to help children suffering the effects of early trauma, abuse or neglect. We conduct research to deepen understanding about the complex needs of these children and how and why these harmful experiences can impair development and lead to social, behavioral and emotional problems. We design and promote research-based models for practical interventions that anyone can use to help children heal and reach their highest potential.*

Rebellion

See chapter 15

Intentional Parenting

Rudeness

Rudeness and vulgarity is common and popularized in movies and television. It is not acceptable in the character of the godly family. Require courtesy in public or at home. Explain what the expected behavior looks like. If violated, have the child start over, back up, and redo what they should have done. Whether it is saying "Please" or "Thank you" or waiting their turn, civility is a must in the well-trained person.

Sass, Back-Talk

See disrespect, Chapter12

Selfishness

No one would deny that we live in a self-oriented culture. Selfishness has risen to even greater heights with the convenience and hobbies of parents taking precedence over the needs and even lives of our children. Now everyone seems to know someone who is an actual narcissist. A friend of mine who works with sex offenders about to get out of prison says it is a universal trait in the incarcerated men he works with.

    Teach your child to consider the feelings of others. Don't let them push ahead of others in line or demand attention at all times. Help them notice and be kind to those who are less fortunate or gifted. Consider sponsoring a child in a third-world country through an organization like Compassion International. Take pre-teens and teens to work at soup kitchens or on short-term mission trips. Help them work for things like electronics rather than feeling they are entitled to the latest gadgets. Teach them to speak the love languages of those in your home. Teach them to share the spotlight and to be content to let others get all the attention at their special times like birthdays.

When I see a child who is quite self-focused and who expects everyone else to focus on them as well, I can't help but think of Baruka (darling) from *Willie Wonka and the Chocolate Factory*. ("I want the world. I want the whole world... Give it to me NOW!") Don't raise a Baruka. Teach your child to put others first.

Sibling Rivalry

Sibling rivalry is as old as the Bible. It puts fear into a mother's heart that her children could actually go as far as Cain and Abel. But before it gets that bad, it is just plain annoying and troubling. The day-to-day picking at each other and pushing each other's emotional buttons wears on a parent. I believe the Bible has answers for us for everyday living. So when my kids were busy with this kind of nonsense, I cried out to the Lord for an answer from scripture. He reminded me of the verse in Proverbs, "Contention comes only by pride." (A plug here, by the way for reading a chapter of Proverbs each day. There are 31 chapters to match the 31 days of a month. I did it several times through to work it deep into my heart and thoughts.) Hmmm, I thought. Pride is it. I'll cure that! I told my children that for every time they kicked each other under the table, or picked on each other, their one-upmanship would get them a consequence of serving that person. The opposite of pride is humility. Serving would bring humility. They would make that person's bed, or rub their back, or carry their dishes to the sink. Their response? "Mom, that's MEAN!" Yup. It worked.

Sitting Still, Inability

One of the skills kids need by the time they go to school is the ability to sit still and concentrate on the task at hand. You might think this is an impossibility for immature little boys, but it is a life skill they will need. Watching television does not count because children's programs change the scene

Intentional Parenting

or the activity in very short increments. There is a lot of flash and dash to draw the child's attention back to the screen if it should wander.

Have young children practice sitting still for as many minutes as they are old, working up to 10 minutes then 15 minutes by the time they are 4 or 5. A friend of mine gives her kids a subject to think about and asks them to sit and ponder quietly. Then at the end of 10 minutes they discuss what they thought about. Pondering, thinking deeply, or mulling things over is another good skill. Train children to sit still through a meal without getting down, running around, or fidgeting.

One warning, if a storm is coming, you will find this task harder than ever to accomplish! With the change of weather, kids get squirrelly. They seem to be about to explode with energy. Just ask any elementary school teacher. Our great-uncle Shorty, who lived with us for four years, was a retired cowboy. He said the little calves kick up their heels when the weather is changing and the frogs croak more. It's just natural. At these times, you may need to send the kids out in the yard and have them run around to blow off their steam. Take a day off from expectations to sit still.

Sneakiness

One of our children enjoyed being sneaky. They were a bit of a spy, but I was also concerned about them getting into trouble with it later in life. I let them know when I noticed they had gotten into the snacks. I also told them I had asked the Lord, who sees everything, to tell me when they were getting into trouble. I don't know how many times the Holy Spirit would nudge me and say, "Go check on them. They're up to something." They wondered how I kept catching them red-handed. With five kids in six years, I needed all the help I could get.

I also told them that if they wanted to be sneaky, they would reap bad consequences. Things have a way of catching up. Of course that happened. And my sneaky child grew up to have one of their own to deal with.

Stealing

You may be shocked and dismayed when your child picks up a package of gum in the grocery store and pockets it. Or perhaps she comes home with a toy from a friend's house. This is certainly evidence that our sinful and selfish natures are alive and well from the get-go. You must deal with this offense immediately. Take your child to return the item.

Intentional Parenting

Have them apologize to the store manager or friend themselves. Do not do it for them. If the child is age 8 or more, you may want to have them work to pay for the item as well. Talk to them about how it feels to be the victim of theft. Make them see beyond their own desires to others' hearts and concerns.

If you are raising a child who has been through neglect and want, such as a foster child, you may find them hoarding food, unsure that you will always consistently provide for them. You may want to have fruit, veggies, or other food they can always access, but you may have to lock up snacks and sweets. Reassure this child that you will be there for them and that food will always be available in your home. This is a special need, and you may need the assistance of a special counselor to help your child get through this problem.

Tattling

One of the more annoying issues parents often deal with is tattling. When our kids approached me to tattle on a sibling, I shut it down right away by asking, "Are they in danger, or are you just trying to get them in trouble?" That usually ended the conversation and they went back to play. Jesus, our big brother is interceding for us, not telling on us. Satan is called "The accuser of the brethren." Don't allow this habit to dominate your family.

Temper Tantrums
See anger chapter.

Unforgiveness
Forgiving is an important part of the correction process. (See Chapter 14.) Those who have been injured must forgive. Some children (and adults) do not find this easy to do. When one child apologizes to another whom they have harmed, the victim must let it go.

Forgiveness means that you release that person from "owing you" for what they did. It does not mean what they did was acceptable or that you deserved it. It does not mean that you automatically trust them again. Reconciliation takes time and is a process. Forgiveness is the first step in a journey.

Remember, Jesus said that if we do not forgive, we cannot be forgiven. Unforgiveness can progress to bitterness, which is a dangerous thing.

Vanity (Vain about looks/beauty)

Our culture is constantly bombarding us with messages that tie beauty and wealth to our personal value. This is wrong. Our value is great because of our Creator's love.

Isaiah 45 says the pot (that which was created – us) cannot say to the potter (the Creator), "Why have you made me this way?" We must accept our unique design with its seeming flaws and strengths as God's design.

What society values in beauty has varied through the centuries. Hundreds of years ago, few people could afford to eat well. People who were plump were considered beautiful, perhaps because it was tied to being wealthy. Today, the rich and famous can use their money to go to spas. They emphasis in on being thin, sometimes abnormally so.

If a child or a young person places their value in beauty, they need to take a look at what happens with age. None of us will be strong and beautiful for our entire lives. We must embrace the seasons.

When I was 30, I did not like how I looked in photos. Now at over 50, I look back and think I looked pretty good. It's all relative. When I bemoaned turning 40, a friend in her 90s said, "Oh, so young."

Intentional Parenting

Things can happen to mar our physical beauty. Illness, injury, and negative emotions. The most beautiful countenance is one aged by peace and confidence in the Lord.

Vengeance

Human tendency is to want vengeance. Early in Genesis, Lamech bragged to his wives about how his vengeance was extra severe - seventy times what the injury was worth. His expression of anger and extreme vengeance is where Jesus' saying comes from about forgiving seventy times seven. Scripture says that vengeance is the Lord's. He is the one who will repay. We are better off to let him judge it. We do not want to reap because we sow something bad while in a vengeful mood. Besides, it's usually the second person who gets caught, right?

With children, there is a need for justice. Parents and adults must be the judge and jury in situations, and ensure that justice for the child is satisfied. If parents do not take care of this, children will grow up with a sense of injury and become bitter and rebellious. Teach your child that you will take care of their need for justice rather than leaving them to think they have to fight for themselves. God certainly does this for us.

Wastefulness

Part of being responsible is being grateful for what we have and using it wisely. When parents provide school supplies, clothing, food, or whatever, it hurts to see it wasted and discarded. Sometimes we have struggled financially and providing has not been easy.

School officials often decry the amount of food that children drop into the trash, in too much of a hurry to eat, or disdaining that which is "healthy." Some parents offer to do lunchroom duty, or ask their children's teacher to watch for this.

If you find yourself having to replace school supplies more frequently than is reasonable, you may want to have your child work for replacements if they have been wasteful. The same is true for hats and gloves. You may need to escort your child to the "Lost and Found" and oversee while they look for their items.

Whining

It's a given fact: a certain percentage of people have melancholy personalities. But that does not mean that children have to grow up being whiny or moody or complaining. One of our children got into this habit around age 3. I'm not sure if he thought it was a way of getting attention, but I decided we were NOT going to live the 15 to 20 years ahead like that! I told him he needed to go back to bed, and he could get up again when he decided to be happy. A few times of that, and he had "reset" his morning behavior. The behavior that gets rewarded, gets repeated.

Sometimes children get fussy when they are overly tired or hungry. Parents must be tuned in to this. Perhaps you need to have a snack handy if lunch will be delayed. Older children can learn to control themselves when they must wait.

What about when they cannot have their way at a friend's house? Teach them to accept others choices at those times and to honor those who are in charge. No child can always have their way or be the most important person in the room everywhere. It's healthy to consider others wishes at times.

Intentional Parenting

Ask yourself, what will this behavior look like in five years? Have I seen this behavior in grown adults? This will motivate you to put the work in to help your child overcome their impulses. Remember, you provide the self-control until they can do it themselves.

Worldliness

Scripture says we are not to be like the world or to love the ways of our culture. Christians should be different than the culture. We cannot love the things of God and love the things of the world.

- What do you value in music? I taught our children to appreciate all different styles of music. We went to the symphony (children's version with explanations), we learned about the lives of all kinds of artists, we listened to all kinds of music. But I drew the line at music with bad lyrics. If the lyrics affirmed sinful behavior or attitudes, it had to go. We did not listen to secular radio (other than instrumental) because of the promotion of wrong behavior and attitudes. See more on this in the Chapter 19 on teens.
- What do you consider important with looks? The world pressures women to all look alike: thin and

big-chested and preferably blonde. I hear women talking to their 10- and 12-year old daughters about dieting. Yikes! Don't start them on that vicious cycle of losing and gaining back weight all their lives! Teach them to eat healthy foods and be active. Teach them to embrace God's design for them – features, body type, and inherited genes.

- What do you value regarding education? Do you focus on getting ahead and making money? Or do you focus on developing the natural gifts and talents within your child?
- What about sexuality? Is the focus on getting a boyfriend or girlfriend? Being wanted, accepted? Or is the focus on purity and preserving their future? We all know people who cannot be happy unless they are in a relationship. Perhaps they are afraid to be alone or perhaps they do not value themselves unless someone else needs or wants them.

We cannot think and act like the world and expect our children to become sweet, godly little Christians. We cannot raise them up to be emotionally stable and wise, yet train them in the ways of our culture. Take a look at the magazine covers in the grocery store and the latest stories on the sad lives of the rich and famous. Look around at people who are focused on having more and forgetting God. What is the fruit in their lives? Intentional parents set a goal for higher things and a better life! It comes from think about how God thinks about things, and applying those principles to our lives.

Worry, Anxiety
Some of us are "world class worriers". I come from a long line of them in my family. For many years I thought I was being responsible through this deep concern and even fearfulness. Then someone shared the scripture with me, "Be anxious for nothing." Yikes! A command! A no-no. Not only had my fearfulness affected my trust in the Lord, it also undermined my confidence in my husband. So I began to practice more prayer, more trust. I would walk myself through the possibilities: What is the *best* case scenario? *Worst* case? Then I realize that real life will fall somewhere in between. I prepared myself as much as I could, and then I told myself that the Lord would help me through whatever came. Mark Twain said, "I've had a lot of worries in my life, most of which never happened." Don't waste your energy and undermine relationships. Learn to trust God.

Intentional Parenting

Help children avoid developing worry habits. Inform them of what is coming ahead of time when possible. Do not talk to them about your fears and concerns. Take those to a trusted friend or counselor. Help them have confidence in the fact that you will take care of them, that you will help them through their difficulties – just like the Lord helps you.

Wrestling

Children, especially boys, like to wrestle. They can be like puppies, playing, rolling around, scrapping, and testing their mettle. This is okay, but often wrestling has no good place to stop. Things tend to escalate until someone gets hurt or angry. This is the point at which adults must stop the wrestling. It has gone from play to anger. As I mentioned earlier, two of my uncles wrestling escalated to the point that one stabbed the other. Wrestling must stop when tempers flair.

Need More Help?

If you find yourself in a long-term, ongoing battle in any one area, you may need the assistance of a professional counselor. For young children, play therapists can draw out a child's concerns that they may not even be able to vocalize. Be sure the counselor you choose is a Christian counselor who shares your values. They should be willing to pray and advise you based on scripture and scriptural principles. There is a difference between truly Biblical counseling and secular counseling, even if the counselor is a Christian.

One of the hard things about parenting is that we are often confronted with our own weaknesses. Maybe one or more of these issues are things YOU need to work on. Look at scripture. Do the work of "put off, put on." Journal. Do a once a month check on the issue. You must be a good example for your child to follow. Do not expect them to be more than what you are. Don't allow yourself to be a do-as-I-say-not-as-I-do parent. This can generate resentment and rebellion in a child. **PUT YOURSELF IN A POSITION TO SUCCEED.**

Endnotes

Ephesians 2:10
Romans 8:29
Colossians 1:10; 1 Thessalonians 4:1; 1 John 3:22
Rev. 22:12
Ephesians 4:29
Genesis 6:11, 13
1 Corinthians 10:10
Philippians 4:8; Matt.6:33; 1 Timothy 1:7
1 Corinthians 15:33
Colossians 3:5, Hebrews 13:5

Intentional Parenting

Exodus 20:17
Proverbs 15:13, 15
Philippians 4:4
Galatians 5:22
1 John 2:9-10
Timothy 6:6
Matthew 12:33
James 4:12 and 5:9
Lying scriptures
Proverbs 29:25
Romans 12:3
Philippians 2:4
Jeremiah 9:24, 1 Corinthians 4:7
Proverbs 16:18 29:23
1 Peter 5:5-6
Isaiah 42:8
Proverbs 13:10
Romans 8:34, Hebrews 7:25
Revelation 12:10
Matthew 6:12
Genesis 4:23
Matthew 18:22
Romans 12:19
Philippians 4:6; Matthew 6:33

Proverbs for Parenting by Barbara Decker. Available through Lynn's Bookshelf. A list of scriptures from the book of Proverbs categorized by behavioral issue.

Chapter 17

What Do Children Need to Learn?

What do our kids need to learn? Everything! From the time they are born until the time they leave home, you will be teaching them all kinds of skills they need in order to be successful adults. There may be some skills that your children will need to learn, but no one taught *you*. I did not develop a consistent personal devotional life until I was in my late 20s. Because it was such a struggle for me, I was determined my children would have that skill under their belts before they left home. Perhaps you wish someone had taught you how to change a flat tire or replace a leaky faucet. You can set your child up for success in life, not only by teaching them the skills you missed, but by instilling confidence in them that they can learn to do things. Those who are capable feel more confident in life.

Remember the line graph from page 133? It helped you understand that you provide the self-control until your child is able to do so on their own. The lighter bands were about teaching your child all the skills they need to succeed in life by the time they leave home.

Intentional Parenting

It's funny how excited we are to teach our kids to walk. We are so patient as they learn. But later, as bigger issues come up, we get uptight.

I would like to recommend one of my favorite books of all time for parents who don't know where to start with teaching kids skills. *401 Ways to Get Your Kids to Work at Home* helped me when I didn't quite know what I should expect from my kids. Their chore chart ideas helped me change things up with each age group. Even before our children could read, we used "Helping Hand Jobs" (wash face, brush teeth, make bed, pick up clothes, pick up toys) with one chore for each finger on a drawing. Later we used the idea of 3 x 5 cards and 2 pockets to move chore items from the "To Do" to the "Done" side. If you only buy one other book on parenting, it should be this one.

Skills List

After the "Helping Hand Jobs" here are some next steps for developing skills. Don't hold back! Prepare them for life. Depending on your child's motor skills and comprehension, you may need to adjust this list a bit. Also, if you have a small family, you will want to rotate the jobs. Don't expect one or two children to do all the chores in a family. If you

Intentional Parenting

have four or more children, you may be able to divide the chores among them, but it is too big a load for one child to do everything.

Toddlers
- ☐ Acknowledge when spoken to (no ignoring)
- ☐ Respond obediently to parents ("quickly & quietly")
- ☐ "Use their words" to communicate (not grunts and pointing or whining).
- ☐ Courteously say hello to someone when introduced
- ☐ Say "please" and "thank you"
- ☐ Share toys joyfully
- ☐ Participate in picking up toys.
- ☐ Going to bed at appointed time. This may be a battle. I used to stand in the hall and put them back in bed over and over until I won and they went to sleep.

Ages 3-5
- ☐ Comb own hair
- ☐ Wash own face
- ☐ Wash self all over thoroughly in bathtub
- ☐ Dress themselves – learning to match clothing
- ☐ Wipe up a spill they have created
- ☐ Put trash in trash can
- ☐ Pick up own toys, put in toy box
- ☐ Clear off own dishes after a meal
- ☐ Fold washcloths or towels to contribute as a family member
- ☐ Courteously say hello to someone when introduced
- ☐ Say "please" and "thank you"

Intentional Parenting

Ages 5-7
- ☐ Set table
- ☐ Clear dishes for guests
- ☐ Organize toys with help, put away toys in appropriate bins or shelves
- ☐ Make own bed (I tied ribbons on the end of their comforters so all they had to do was pull everything up.)
- ☐ Leave the bathroom tidy after they use it
- ☐ Put away own clean clothes (carefully)
- ☐ Shake small area rugs
- ☐ Spot clean walls or woodworks with spray and a rag
- ☐ Feed pets (We required that this be done before they ate their own breakfast. Pets are helpless.)
- ☐ Wash sinks including doing a good job around the faucet
- ☐ Sweep porches, patios, and sidewalks
- ☐ Wipe off chairs in kitchen
- ☐ Unload dishwasher – items they can reach or that are not too heavy. One note, make sure you first take out the things you don't want to have broken. From time to time kids may drop and break things. Plan to react calmly and help clean up. You may want to invest in unbreakable melamine dishes for a while.
- ☐ Money – understand penny, dime, nickel, quarter and denominations of paper money.
- ☐ Savings vs. spending. We used a simple plan for our kids when they were young: 10% tithe (giving to God), 10% saving (a piggy bank) and they could spend the rest. We discussed wisdom with spending such as buying things that last vs. candy or junk.

Ages 8-10

- ☐ Wash own hair
- ☐ Wash combs and brushes
- ☐ Trim own nails
- ☐ Fold and put away towels
- ☐ Sort laundry for washing (whites, darks, colors, delicates)
- ☐ Fold clothes neatly and put away where they belong
- ☐ Organize own drawers, closet with help
- ☐ Clean mirrors (and TV screen if you are willing)
- ☐ Clean toilets, including doing a good job around the base.
- ☐ Empty wastebaskets, take out trash, put in liner bags
- ☐ Understand use of different household cleaners – for example using disinfectant cleaners in bathrooms and kitchens. Note the caution on the bottles and teach them not to mix chemicals. (Bleach + other cleaners gives of toxic gas.)
- ☐ Load dishwasher - including understanding how the arms spray so they load in the most effective ways.
- ☐ Hand wash and dry dish items that do not go in the dishwasher. Understand special cleaning instructions for non-stick pans or delicate dishes.
- ☐ Sweep (with broom) or vacuum floors. Explain how to "edge" with either.
- ☐ Dust furniture
- ☐ Continue money skills plus teach them how to properly count back change (Nearly a lost art!)
- ☐ Open a savings account. Keep a passbook (like a check register).
- ☐ Manners and courtesy

Intentional Parenting

- ☐ How to introduce people who do not know one another. How to graciously meet new people.

Ages 10-14
- ☐ Hang clothes on clothesline for drying
- ☐ Polish own shoes - lay out a newspaper, use liquid or wax type polish, buff after drying
- ☐ How to iron clothing. (One of our girls did ironing for extra money!)
- ☐ Changing sheets, remaking beds
- ☐ Folding sheets and blankets neatly
- ☐ Picking up trash in the yard (including "pooper scooper" if you have pets. Have them wear gloves or put a trash bag over their hand or use a shovel, then wash hands.) There is responsibility in having pets!
- ☐ Clean entire bathroom including tub
- ☐ Polish wood or glass furniture
- ☐ Mop floors using appropriate cleaners
- ☐ Clean pet cages and bowls
- ☐ Take written phone messages accurately
- ☐ Vacuum upholstery (and under couch cushions)
- ☐ How to empty the vacuum canister or change a vacuum bag. Show them how the belt works.
- ☐ Water house plants (amounts and frequency)
- ☐ Water lawn, outside plants
- ☐ Wash the car, vacuuming it out, cleaning windows
- ☐ Weed garden
- ☐ Changing light bulbs, understanding different kinds of bulbs, wattage and lumens
- ☐ Polishing silver
- ☐ How to oil a squeaky door

- ☐ Beginning cooking skills (see below)
- ☐ Basic nutrition and eating a balanced diet. (I prefer the old basic four food groups to the new, more complicated pyramid!) How many servings of each needed for growing teens? Portion sizes. What do calories mean?
- ☐ Continue money skills. Help them consider increasing their savings for larger purchases.
- ☐ How to return an item to the store.
- ☐ Swimming (If they haven't already learned how.)
- ☐ Internet use and safety. This is a good thing to discuss as a family. Consider the internet safety pledge found at www.safefamilies.org.
- ☐ Teamwork. We homeschooled our kids. Homeschooled kids tend to be good individual workers, but you have to create opportunities for them to learn teamwork.
- ☐ Listening skills. Others have important things to impart. Older adults have interesting experiences they are often willing to talk about if someone will listen. They have knowledge and skills that your child might need if they are willing to draw that person out. Proverbs 20:5 says (my paraphrase), "Good advice from a wise person is like a deep well. If you are wise you will draw it out."

Ages 15-18

- ☐ Arrange for own haircuts
- ☐ Purchase own grooming supplies (I had my kids use their own money so they could choose whatever they liked and were willing to pay for.)
- ☐ Waterproof own shoes or boots

Intentional Parenting

- ☐ Do own laundry. You must teach them stain removal (pretreating with spray or using Biz or Tri-Zyme from Amway in the wash), how to read labels for washing instructions, and fabric content. Teach them how to hand wash delicate items.

    Some people do this younger, but I was not willing to buy clothes to replace their "mistakes". At this age they had babysitting money or odd jobs money to pay for their own clothing from time to time.

    Don't forget to teach them to clean the lint trap in the dryer.

    Talk about per-use costs of various soaps and why you use what you use.

    Discuss what dry cleaning is and what items require that type of cleaning.
- ☐ Basic mending by hand – rips, sewing on buttons
- ☐ Machine sewing
- ☐ How to shop for clothing. What fabrics wear well, why designer brands are overpriced, how to decide what is worth paying for. Thrift store and consignment store shopping. Comparing how long things will last and whether the thrift store item is really a bargain.

    I taught my kids the "Rule of 3". The item you buy must go with 3 items of clothing or be able to be worn in 3 ways. This means their money will go farther.

    Discuss how much an item costs per wearing. Can it be worn many times or will it be worn to only once? Is that the way they want to spend their money? Maybe that prom dress should come from a consignment shop instead.

Intentional Parenting

- Items that have to be dry cleaned will probably be worn less often.
- ☐ Grocery shopping including understanding unit pricing, different cuts of meat.
- ☐ How to use (or not use) coupons. Discuss whether the item is something you would normally buy or not. Is it a new product you want to try?
- ☐ Understanding how advertising works and appeals to emotions and creates peer pressure.
- ☐ How to clean drapes and blinds
- ☐ How to clean a refrigerator, defrost a freezer
- ☐ Spring/fall cleaning – baseboards, windows, carpets, etc. twice a year.
- ☐ Lawn care including mowing, edging, fertilizing, weed killers
- ☐ Cleaning fireplace and the need for a chimney sweep
- ☐ How to check for tripped breakers (electrical box). Fuses in cars, etc.
- ☐ How to change a vacuum belt
- ☐ How to trim trees and shrubs
- ☐ How to unstop a drain using a plunger or chemical drain opener
- ☐ How to wax a floor
- ☐ How to paint a room (leaving no thin spots)
- ☐ How to replace a faucet or put in a new washer
- ☐ How to caulk (tubs, sinks, and weatherizing)
- ☐ How to shop for home appliances
- ☐ How to use public transportation
- ☐ How to read a map
- ☐ How to clean a stove and oven (Be careful to examine manufacturer's instructions so you don't void a warranty.)

- How to write a check, how to balance a checkbook each month. How to use a debit card.
- How to make online purchases. Watching for security protocols.
- How to plan a party (Who and how many to invite, food, games, decorations)
- Uses of basic (over the counter) medication
- How to find what we need (including free how-to classes at the library and home improvement stores!)
- Test-taking (Many people have test anxiety. Help your child see this as a snapshot in time of their abilities. They want to show what they know, but it is not life or death! This anxiety can be overcome.)
- How to carry on a conversation (two-sided!). How to make small talk. One easy way to think of something to talk about is the simple acronym F-O-R-M.

  F is for *Family*. Ask about their background, do they have any siblings, what they do as a family, what they remember from their childhood, and so on.

  O is for *Occupation*. What do they do for work? (adults) Do they babysit or do odd jobs? (kids their age) What is their job like? (adults)

  R is for *Recreation*. What do they do for fun? Do they have hobbies? Do they like to camp or read? Do they work out? Do they compete in athletic event?

  M is for *Message*. Do you have a message or information you want to get across? Is there something you especially want them to know about you? Is there an issue you want to talk to this person about? Now is a good time to bring that up – after you've been a good listener and drawn them out.

Intentional Parenting

- ☐ Philanthropy, volunteer service. This is good to do both individually and as a family. Let your child choose what they want to be involved in. Don't volunteer them to babysit for others. Let them choose where to serve.
- ☐ Understand and have self-discipline, self-motivation. For some this comes more naturally than for others. If it is not a personal strength, work on developing it.
- ☐ Scheduling, time-management
- ☐ Goal setting (personal growth, spiritually, financially, etc.)
- ☐ Touch typing ("Keyboarding" they call it since the advent of the computer.)
- ☐ Basic computer skills – MS Word, email, internet use at a minimum. Excel is a great addition. Check with your local library for free classes!
- ☐ How to drive (not that you are going to have to bring this up!)

Ages High School to Adult
- ☐ How and when to use credit. Understanding the pressure and tactics credit card companies apply to get you in debt to them. Understanding that they will extend more credit than you can really afford – enough so you can make payments, but never pay off. (Revolving credit) Consider a Dave Ramsey teen course.
- ☐ Understanding household budgeting (rent or mortgage, utilities, insurances, phone, groceries, gasoline, car maintenance, etc.) and paying bills.
- ☐ What it costs to get an apartment (including deposits, renters' insurance, etc.) How to arrange for utilities (another deposit) and trash service.

Intentional Parenting

        Having an old-fashioned "hope chest" is great for girls. Boys need to understand what they will need to set up housekeeping on their own if they are not married. (Dishes, towels, blankets, and so on.)
- What vacations cost (and inexpensive options)
- How to contact a landlord about a problem
- How to figure gasoline mileage
- Cost of (and paying for) own auto insurance
- Basic auto maintenance – how to check fluid (including testing radiator fluid before winter), how to check tire pressure and change a flat. How to change oil if you do your own. A huge plus would be understanding how the different systems of a car work. (Bonus points!)
- How to drive a car with a manual transmission (stick shift). A must for everyone! Find a patient teacher who really explains how this works! If you can drive a stick shift, you will be more confident driving ANYTHING! (Or challenged if you can't!)
- First Aid – whether you go into the medical field or become a parent you WILL use this skill!
- Understanding different personality types – strengths and weaknesses.
- How to get along with people who are different than you
- What to look for in a mate
- Decision-making skills
- Conflict resolution skills. Certainly there are plenty of opportunities to practice this with siblings. Life will always have difficult situations that must be addressed. They happen in the workplace, they happen in marriages, they happen in families. Being able to talk things through calmly, to discuss what one

Intentional Parenting

needs in a situation, having fair and reasonable expectations, is a skill that will take anyone far. You must be willing to enter that "tunnel of chaos" to have the difficult discussion. It's the only way to get to the other side. Don't let your young person put off dealing with things. Avoidance doesn't work.

- Ability to receive constructive criticism. This means they must be teachable and willing to accept whatever portion of the criticism is true. One wise teacher said, "Own your 10%" – or 30% or 60%.
- Having an honest view of themselves – their skills and abilities, strengths and weaknesses.
- Proper ways of deriving self-worth (more on this in the chapter on teens.)
- Thinking analytically, logically. Seeing fallacies in arguments and discussions.
- Clear understanding of people's actions and motivations for what they do.
- Choosing a career that fits with their talents, personality and interests. I especially like the curriculum *Career Choices* by Mindy Bingham and Sandy Stryker, published by Academic Innovations. It asks, "Who am I?" "What do I want?" and "How do I get it?" There is good material on deciding what is really important in life.

Learning for YOU

What about those skills on this list that YOU haven't learned? You may find yourself learning right along with your child. Check with your local library for classes and resources. Ours offers some basic computer how-to classes, and they will

Intentional Parenting

know where to find more. We also took a great "How to Lay Tile" class with our daughter and son-in-law at a local Home Depot store. Need to fix a faucet or re-program your garage door opener? There is probably a YouTube video for nearly everything.

derEx*cellence*

Teach your children to do things with excellence. Do not accept sloppy work from them. If they skim through in cleaning the bathroom, inspect it. Have them come back to redo around the base of the toilet or behind the faucet. Set the standard high so they will not be embarrassed if they do the same job for a living at some point. Of course this takes more of your time at first, but it will pay off in the long run. Several of our daughters have worked in jobs where they had to train younger people. They were appalled at the high percentage of high school-aged kids who had never mopped a floor or never done dishes by hand. This is debilitating to the teenager. Teach them, even if it is easier to do it yourself. By the time they are teenagers you will find your load lightened, and you won't shudder and wonder how they will survive on their own.

A friend of mine once said, "Children don't do what we *expect*, but what we *inspect*." True that. You will have to follow up on other things like homework and what they did while at their friend's house, and so on. Parenting is hard work. Embrace it.

One aspect of excellence is being a "finisher." Many people are content to start projects, but not finish. First one must count the cost when starting, making sure that it will be possible to complete the project. Jesus talked about this. In our city there is a shell of a mall that was begun and not finished. It just sits there, a testament to someone's inability to plan well and finish. Rewards come, not in the middle of projects, but when they are finished. It takes patience and perseverance to finish, both good character traits.

Do-It-Yourself

The temptation in all this is to do all the housework and the yard work and the cooking yourself. First of all, it's easier. Training your children takes time. Inspecting their work takes time. You may feel guilty, thinking it's really *your* job. Sometimes you just want to get it done and out of the way. My husband made a very specific request on this, which at the time dismayed me. "If the children can learn to do it, I do not want you doing it." Yikes! That was tough! But he was right! Our oldest child was then about eight. Over the years our kids learned to do every facet of housework and most kinds of small repairs and home maintenance. We are so glad my husband took leadership in this way and helped and encouraged me to follow through.

A healthy side-effect of training your children is to create some good boundaries for Mom. You may not know anyone like this (wink, wink, nudge, nudge), but there are moms who are like slaves to their families. Really! They make the mad dash to get the cookies for the scout meeting that Junior failed to inform Mom about. (Even though he'd known his turn was coming for two weeks.) They drop their agenda for the day in order to make up the difference for every needy person who calls. They pick up around the house while their families sit on the couch watching TV. Sometimes moms need training too. I remember the day I found the quote, "Failure to plan on your part, does not constitute an emergency on my part." I wrote it out and posted it above my desk. Wow! It was like being given permission to say no, which was a skill which I sadly lacked. We instituted the rule that kids needed to give adults 24 hours' notice (except in emergencies). If they needed goodies or wanted to have a friend over after Sunday church, they needed to plan ahead. It was a relief for me, and a new skill for them. And it was more respectful of one another.

Cooking Skills List

My mother could not cook when she got married. She had worked outside the home and helped with the family income, so her mother felt bad about having her help around the house. Mom found herself at a disadvantage as a newlywed, so she began teaching me to cook and follow recipes when I was seven or eight.

Several of my kids' friends ate poorly after they left home, surviving on an imbalanced diet of canned tuna and Hamburger Helper. One became seriously ill as a result and was even hospitalized. Here is the list of what I taught my kids to cook. From here they could tackle anything they wanted to in the kitchen. They have amazed me a number of times, and I've eaten some wonderful meals at their homes as a result of their skills. They also are capable in the area of entertaining and hospitality as a result. They make me smile.

Cooking Requirements

Cooking terms such as bake, broil, simmer, etc.

Intentional Parenting

Food safety (germs, hot/cold temps to avoid food poisoning, how to know if food is spoiled) I recommend the Colorado State University Extension Service's website for all kinds of useful food safety info!

Understanding different cuts of meat and for what they are best used

Reading labels, understanding dyes, additives, artificial sweeteners

How to make:
    Two kinds of soup
    Biscuits
    Muffins
    Yeast Bread – how yeast works
    Eggs – how to make several types, how long to boil (different at high altitude), know terms such as over-easy, over-medium, etc.
    Roast (with potatoes, carrots and gravy)
    Fried chicken, gravy (You may want to include how to cut up a chicken, which is a lost art.)
    Baked chicken
    1 or 2 casseroles
    Veggies – fresh and cooked. Know food value, vitamins in the food
    Baked, mashed potatoes
    3 kinds of cookies
    1 pie
    Punch for a party
    2 kinds of hors d'oeuvres
    Coffee
    Iced tea

By the time your child learns to do these, they will have the ability to read any recipe and the confidence to try lots of new things in cooking.

Creativity vs. TV

Another good skill to teach children is how to play creatively without having the TV on. Teach them to use their imagination. Show them how to turn the bunk beds into a tent, how to make a fort or a hideout, how to notice things in nature. My kids loved *The Boys Handy Book* and *The Girls Handy Book* reprinted from the 1882 and 1887 versions.

TV is often the cheap answer for boredom. Our kids learned not to say, "I'm bored!" Rather than let them trap me into conjuring up fun ideas and being their entertainment coordinator, I said if they were bored I would come up with an extra chore or more school work. For example, they could help me mate socks from the everlasting sock box. Needless to say, they became very good at thinking up something fun to do, usually together.

We chose to limit our children's TV time to 1 ½ hours per day. Perhaps you would want to include all media time, like for video games. For several years, the kids got 21

Intentional Parenting

poker chips, or "TV tokens," at the beginning of the week. Each represented ½ hour of TV time. They had to pay to watch TV. If they wanted to watch a 2-hour movie (other than one I dictated for family time all together), it cost them 4 tokens. If they had a favorite show, they might need to set aside tokens early in the week to make sure they didn't run out before it came on. Needless to say, they became more choosey about what they watched. This was most effective in the later elementary to early middle school years.

Endnotes

401 Ways to Get Your Kids to Work at Home by Bonnie McCullough and Susan Monson

The American Boy's Handy Book by Daniel Beard and Noel Perrin – a reproduction of the 1880s book

The American Girls Handy Book by Lina Beard and Adelia Beard – a reproduction of the 1880s book

Chapter 18
Spiritual Life

It is common in our culture to hear people say, "Don't impose your values on me." They don't even think parent should impose their values on their children. They may say, wait until they grow up so they can decide for themselves. This is foolish. Parents should teach children what they need to know. No wonder we have such a godless society.

First of all, faith is more caught than taught. Parents must model faith as a walk or a way of life. It is a journey of learning and growing. Your child should see you learning and growing. You should tell them about the things you are praying for. You should pray together for things that concern the family. They should see that you enjoy your journey of faith. As any other part of life that we've talked about so far, kids have an advantage if they start young and are trained by those who are experienced in good things. That should be YOU!

From there, begin to read Bible stories to your children and discuss them. Whether you use the actual Bible or a Bible story book, teach them that the Word of God is true. These are not fables, they are history. The Bible is not a collection of beliefs invented my man, but God connecting to humans because He loves us. There is more evidence for the accuracy of the Bible and for the existence of Jesus Christ than there is for Julius Caesar or Shakespeare.

Teach your children that God is the Creator of all things and as such He owns everything. He is the "boss" of it all. He is grieved when people misuse His gifts. I love the verse in Isaiah that tells how God could have made the earth a wasteland for us, but instead He gave us all the beauty around us.

Teach them that because of man's sin in the Garden things are now less than perfect. We battle sin. Bad things happen in the world. God doesn't like it either, and eventually He will clean it all up. For now He is letting mankind reap what we have sown from our mutiny against Him.

Explain the salvation story – how Jesus came to earth so that we could understand and connect with God. He meant to have a relationship with us, His creation. Due to the fall, we are separate from God by sin. It is the Grand Canyon between us and God. It is too big to jump over. We need Jesus' sacrifice for our sin to restore us to relationship with God. Because of the fall, all human beings are born with a sin nature. We fight temptation. We struggle against sin and wrong choices.

Jesus was the Son of God and yet He was like us. He lived a normal life, but never sinned. He loved humankind so much that he was willing to die a horrible death to pay for our sins. God raised him from the dead. Jesus conquered death itself. Someday those who believe these things will get to be in heaven with God. We will be rewarded for our deeds, but they do not save us. If they did, Jesus would not have had to die.

Teach your children that God loves us and is involved with and concerned about our lives. He sees us. He has a plan for us. He wants us to become more like his son.

Age of Accountability

I was raised to believe that there was an "age of accountability" or a time of maturity at which children can truly understand spiritual things. It was thought to be around 12 years old. Perhaps adults were wanting kids to have a fuller understanding of faith matters or perhaps it was connected to the story of young Jesus in the temple. I have found that young children, often as young as 3 or 4, can understand the plan of salvation and pray to accept Christ as

Lord (a.k.a. boss) of their lives. They can pray and have faith for answers to prayer. They can talk to others about Jesus. They can converse with adults about faith matters. I believe children as young as 6 or 7 can understand water baptism, communion, and other matters of faith.

Then each child has the opportunity to make daily choices about how they are going to live. They will choose to be obedient or disobedient. They will choose to act on impulses or be more deliberate in their choices. You must impress on them the importance of making those good decisions.

They will need to be encouraged to have their own devotional life (prayer, Bible reading, Bible study, memorizing scripture) and walk out spiritual disciplines (serving others, finding and walking out their life callings, fasting, pondering scriptural principles, spiritual growth.)

Making Faith Their Own

For children who grow up in a Christian home, there will come a time that they have to grapple with turning their family beliefs into personal beliefs. This often happens in the teen years. Kids may wonder if they might have grown up in a family that was in a cult. They may search scriptures or read doctrinal books to validate what they have been taught. Or they may wrestle with the lure of worldly things and whether they want to follow Christ after all.

I made a firm decision to walk with the Lord for the rest of my life in about third grade. I pondered whether to be like others or to be a Christian (I did not know of any believers in my class). I knew I would be so miserable without Christ. Then in my junior year in high school, I needed to examine what I had been taught and weigh it critically. Several of my children went through this around age 14. They were making an adult choice, and whether they define it as "getting saved," coming to Christ for the first time, or making a more definite commitment, it is something they had to work through personally. It is important that you don't try to "fix" their thinking and hurt them. Accept their perceptions unless they are dangerous or seriously unbiblical. Give them room to grow. If you push or try to control this, they will feel misunderstood and the enemy will whisper things that can stir resentment or rebellion.

Do as I Do

My dad has a favorite saying, "Talk is cheap." Parents, it is easy to tell your kids what to do and live differently yourself.

When I teach parenting classes and ask for a show of hands for how many adults grew up in an environment of "Do as I say, not as I do," a majority of hands go up. Kids are watching when you gossip about others, when you get something at the grocery story they forgot to put on your bill, and when you say go to church but stay home. They see when you cheat on your taxes but tell them not to cheat on a test. They see when you speed but tell them to obey the laws.

    I guarantee you that this does not work. Let me repeat, THIS DOES NOT WORK!!

    While you cannot be perfect, you can show your child that you are learning from the Bible and trying to put it into practice. You can tell them you felt convicted about something you did and let them see you apologize and correct the error.

    Over and over we see that our kids are like us. When they repeat that off-color story and we are embarrassed or when they yell at their dolls, we know they are walking out our example.

    Recently, my husband asked our children what they remembered and what they thought about having grown up as PK's – Pastor's Kids. One thing that came up again and again was thankfulness that what they saw at church in us was

Intentional Parenting

no different from what they saw in us at home. That consistency was important to them in making it easy for them to embrace a Christian life. Now they shine as they stand on our shoulders. We are so often impressed with them and their walks of faith. They are better parents and better Christians than we were at their age.

Personal Devotions
I shall probably never forget the day when my 10-year old son said to his grumpy mother, "Mom, have you had your devotions today?" I mumbled that I had not, and that I would excuse myself, go to my room and get them done. He knew that these things were connected because I had told him so. I had also worked with him about his need for being faithful with "devoes". He had experience the same thing, and knew what he was seeing.

It is good to have family devotions, but it does not replace individual devotions. Kids need individual devotional times, too. They need to develop it as a habit, just as you would impart the habit to brush their teeth before they go to bed. As soon as our children could read a little, we got them picture Bibles. They were a bit like a comic book Bible. When they began to read well, we got them NIV Bibles with

Intentional Parenting

larger print that they could read on their own. I wanted something with everyday language they could understand. There are also so many lovely children's Bibles. Some even have craft project ideas in them. Currently I am reading the New Living Translation through (and loving it) to get a fresh perspective on familiar scriptures. It is well written in everyday language, without being a paraphrase that loses deep meaning.

    I frequently asked our children what they were reading in the Bible and what it meant to them personally. Was there anything they felt God was speaking to them about? I taught them to listen for the quiet impressions in their heart that come from the Holy Spirit. I asked if they needed a devotional book. (I highly recommend *Made to Shine, a Girls Only Devotional* by our friends The Sonflowerz!) I would be glad to purchase whatever they needed to keep this moving forward.

    Through all this we taught our kids that their Christian walk was their own relationship with the God of the Universe. He wanted to know them and speak to them. He would help them with problems. He had a destiny for them. If they were obedient, available and teachable He would reveal His wonderful path for them.

Applying Scripture

My husband and I taught our children that God's Word, the Bible, was authoritative. It was God speaking to humankind. It was to be obeyed. It was not just a collection of wise writings. It had answers for everyday life. We looked to scripture for examples and explanations about life. When we evaluated what was going on around us, we looked at how God felt about this kind of situation.

Memorizing Scripture

In the recesses of my mind there is a treasure box full of the verses I memorized as a child in Sunday School. "Be sure, your sin will find you out," Psalm 23, and so many others. I remember a babysitter who made us learn verses like the Lord's Prayer and the Beatitudes at 4 and 5 years old. Memorization is easiest for children in the elementary grades. What a good time to fill the treasure box of their minds. If you need some ideas for this, take a look at the A-B-C list in Appendix 2.

Another favorite thing of mine is scripture songs. During the 1970's and 80's a lot of choruses were written that were scriptures put to music. Those are in my mind as well.

Intentional Parenting

You can purchase CD's of these older songs and there are some great scripture CD's for children specifically.

Recently I was chatting with a friend and fondly remembering *Music Machine,* a musical story about the Fruit of the Spirit, and *Antsylvania,* an ant story full of puns and expressive words about the prodigal son (in this case an ant.)

Prayer

Prayer is talking to God. God listens. He cares and He is all-powerful when it comes to answering. We may not always understand, but He does answer. (Sometimes the answer is "no".) Prayer should be our first response to bad news or problems that arise. We should pray about everything. We should pray for our needs and for the needs of others. Our children should see us living this as a way of life.

Prayer is more than asking for "stuff". It is also asking God what is important to Him in situations and in the world. We should prayerfully make His main thing our main thing.

Living Counter-Culturally

If you haven't noticed it by now, living an active, real Christian life is counter-cultural. The world would like us to

Intentional Parenting

keep this to ourselves, and better yet, keep it at church on Sunday.

Scripture says if we really love God, we do not go on sinning. If we live this out, it is definitely going to stand out. If we make our choices in light of our values, there will be a number of things we choose not to do. Not because we can't, but because we don't want to. Violent movies, sexualized TV shows, irreverent and ungodly music will not be enjoyable. Worldly interests will not benefit us. Our identity will be established in what we like, in what we enjoy. Evil things should turn our spiritual stomachs.

Living Paradoxically

Living paradoxically means embracing the world of opposites from scripture: the kind are more blessed than the powerful. The poor in spirit get to see God. It is more blessed to give than receive. To be a leader you must serve.

The Bible is full of these ideas. (You can read more if in *Willmington's Book of Bible Lists* or look it up on the internet.) Christians find the tensions between the world's values and God's frequently conflicting. Embracing God's priorities takes work and practice. It certainly goes against the flow of what is thought to be "normal." It changes our priorities.

Teachable Moments

In the Old Testament parents are commanded to talk to their kids about God's ways when they sit down, when they get up in the morning, when they walk (or drive) down the road, and as they are going about their day. We had many wonderful conversations with our kids throughout their preteen and teen years about topics that would just pop up at odd moments. Once, while driving by a place the kids had seen on TV as the location of a shooting in our city, we had a huge discussion about crime and what the Bible says about capital punishment. It came out of nowhere.

In these moments you can share what scripture says, how God feels about the problem, what he wants believers to do about the pain in the world and so on. Sin fills our world with so much trouble and pain. God lets mankind be in charge of a lot. Redemption can change that if people will respond and do right. If your child asks questions for which you don't know the answer, tell them you will look up answers and discuss it further in a day or two. (Be sure to follow through!)

Even young children understand more than you think. They are thinking and evaluating everything around them. They are pondering why you were short with your spouse. They are considering why you seem not to like that person down the street. It's best to talk things through with them than to let them figure it out – and get it wrong.

Also, some young children want to be in the know about everything. They see themselves as the family detective. One of our children, without our knowing it, read the faxes that came in at our house during a church crisis. We didn't know they were doing this until years later. Their conclusions were not completely correct, but they were sure better informed than we thought! It's better to inform children and tell them what you want them to know than to let them fill in the blanks themselves.

Attending Church

We attended church as a family. We talked about it together. This was a part of the fabric of our home. We did it because we wanted to be a part of a community of believers. If you are looking for a good church, take a look at Appendix 1 for ideas of what to look for in a healthy church.

Intentional Parenting

On the way to church I talked to our young ones about what to expect. There would be singing and I wanted them to stand when everyone stood. I would hold the youngest and say the words quickly into her ear so she could sing along with us.

I wanted our children to participate and pay attention. (Remember, what you *allow* is trained in.) So when it was time for the sermon they were to listen while they wrote or drew.

Once the kids moaned that they would be too tired to stand and participate. I reminded them that Jesus was tired while he was dying on the cross for them. Their excuses did not hold water with me.

What about putting small children in the nursery? This is fine for a season, but the ultimate goal is for them to be able to sit and learn in church. Think about when you will work on that.

What about children who won't stay in the nursery? First of all, this is your decision, not theirs. You have to be prepared to enforce your decision. One of our children especially disliked being in nursery. We had been through the crying fits and long battles over it. Finally, I said to him, if you can sit still by me, you may stay in the service. If you get fidgety or noisy, you go to nursery, no arguments. He learned to sit still for 10-15 minutes, then was ready to go to nursery. Later, he could sit still all through worship. Eventually, he did not need nursery at all, which was fine with both of us.

Part of my concern was that I get some time to worship and listen and a break from 5 children under 6. I also needed some adult conversation, as you might imagine. Training our children to participate in a service was a long-term process. It often involved sacrifice on my part.

What about teen and youth groups? More about that in the chapter on teens. For your adult children who live with you – see Chapter 20 on adult children.

The Truth about Heaven and Hell
Scripture is very clear about Heaven (or the New Heaven and New Earth) and Hell (eternal punishment). It is also clear about rewards or punishment for our works. While I would not tell very young children about the frightful details of hell, we must remember it was not made for human beings to start with. I would emphasize how obedience makes us happy, disobedience is sad and weighs us down.

Again, this is about God being in charge, about His plan being in place. Judgment and punishment are not meant for human beings, but we have a free will and may choose. God is obligated to keep His word and follow through.

You may run into the difficult question of where did Aunt Tillie (who was mean and unsaved) go? Rather than avoiding the question or bending the truth, you may want to answer with something like, "She will face God to talk about what she was like and whether she had accepted Jesus."

Spiritual Disciplines

It is wise to teach your children about spiritual disciplines like fasting as you are involved with it. Several times there were all-church fasts we participated in, and I prepared food for the children like a "Daniel fast". That meant beans and vegetables and tofu instead of normal foods for a day or two. When they were older they could choose what level of participation they would like to do.

Other disciplines such as meditation, service, simplicity and study are discussed in *The Celebration of Discipline*. As you grow in these areas yourself, discuss them with your kids and how they can apply these truths at their age. Don't say they aren't old enough to understand. You'd be surprised at how much they can get.

The Fear of the Lord

The Fear of the Lord and the love of God are two sides of the same coin. Just as we love and honor our parents, we have a healthy concern for displeasing them. We know that if we are rebellious, there will be tough times ahead. I remember misbehaving once in church, and my dad looking down the pew and giving me "the look." In the car after church, he said, "We'll talk about it when we get home." Uh-oh. I knew I was in big trouble. That's like the fear of the Lord. It is more than respect.

I recommend John Bevere's DVD series and workbook called, *The Fear of the Lord*. Do it with your teenagers. Share it with their grandparents. It will change how you see many things. John especially covers the difference between being afraid of the Lord and a proper "fear of the Lord."

Secularism, Humanism and "Science"

There is so much pressure to remove spiritual things from the public square. Thinking spiritually is unwelcome. There is much pressure to keep your to yourself. Universities teach that men have made up religion. Evolution and humanism are the religion of our day. And it's not working.

Teach your children to think critically. At the Museum of Natural History they need to learn to say, "How do you know that?" when the sign says millions and millions of years. True science is reproducible and observable. It takes a lot of faith to believe in evolution. People who want to believe in anything but God go to great lengths to explain Him away. Teach your kids to see that these theories keep changing. They are full of errors. The models have to be removed because they've made things up that didn't really exist. See what the Institute for Creation Research has to say.

Summit Ministries in Manitou Springs, Colorado has a worldview conference and great resources to teach your kids how to think in this secularist environment. Consider this or a similar course for your high schoolers. Read Christian apologetics and books such as *Evidence that Demands a Verdict*. Christianity is actually <u>more</u> logical than secularism. Teach your kids to think.

Endnotes

Isaiah 45:18.
Gen. 3; Romans 5:12-21
Psalm 139
Jeremiah 29:11
Romans 8:29; Ephesians 2:10
The phrase "Making His main thing our main thing" comes from *The Fear of the Lord* by John Bevere.

Intentional Parenting

Hebrews 10:26
Heaven and Hell   Matthew 25, Luke 16:19-31, Revelation 20:11-15
Rewards   Rev 22:12
Renewal Ministries of Colorado Springs   www.renewalcs.org has many resources and Biblical teachings.
Celebration of Discipline by Richard J. Foster
Institute for Creation Research   www.icr.org
Worldview - Summit Ministries   www.Summit.org
Apologetics – *The New Evidence that Demands a Verdict* by Josh McDowell
   See also *The Truth Project* from **Focus on the Family**
Made to Shine, A Girls Only Devotional by Becca Leander Nicholson and Elissa Leander Tipps – The Sonflowerz   www.Sonflowerz.com

Chapter 19

Making the Teen Years Great

If you just picked up this book and turned to this chapter first, you are not alone. When I ask the parents in my *Intentional Parenting* classes what they are most concerned about, the teen years top the list every time. They may fear the teenage rebellion that is proverbial and accepted in our culture. I disagree that it is to be expected. Parents may be dealing with the cultural norm that lets kids spend hours on video games and personal pleasure and wonder how to get their teens to engage with the family and have better character.

Our kids' teen years were not without challenge and fearful moments, but I would have to say most of the problems we experienced were tied to things we had already been dealing with. The child who had been strong-willed before was strong-willed as a teen. The child who had been more interested in socializing with people other than family members had some similar issues as a teen.

Again and again the lives of our children, and later our teens are made up of choices. Will you follow the Lord's

Intentional Parenting

path to a blessed life, or will you choose another path and the pain and heartache that go with it?

Parental Posture

Some parents are so uptight about the teen years that they change in how they deal with their kids at this season. They may feel uncomfortable letting their 14-year old daughter sit on their lap or hold their hand at the ballgame. They may overreact in fear to discipline issues. Some parents lecture their children on and on, trying to impart that which they've not taught or modeled in the past. They are "cramming" for the coming day of their child leaving home. These kinds of behaviors will hurt and confuse kids. Get a grip and maintain the solid way you have been parenting all along. (If you haven't already created family goals, back up to chapter 9 and start there.)

I often see two extremes in the way parents handle themselves in relating to their teens. One is to smother them, keeping a tight grip and controlling everything they can in their child's life. This kind of parent is fearful of the child making mistakes, perhaps expensive ones. They put off allowing the child to ease into adult activities (like driving) or hold out on letting them make their own choices (like clothing). These parents don't let their teens have enough freedom, and this sets the child up to rebel, perhaps even run away. Sometimes these are the kids who go crazy and throw off *all* restraint after they leave home.

The other extreme is the parent who is too trusting or too busy to stay on top of what is going on with their teen and his friends. Their parenting is loose and free. Perhaps they want to be their child's buddy. (That should come later.) Or perhaps they are too unsure of themselves to be firm in training or guiding their teens. The teen may love it, but the parent is in for ugly surprises. Teens do not have the maturity to make big life decisions without adult input and oversight. Be advised that you are legally and financially responsible for what your underage children do. (You also have a right to be present if they are questioned by authorities.)

Get Ready

Here are some things you WILL have to deal with during the teen years:

Intentional Parenting

Fear of Being Different

Nearly all teens are afraid of standing out. The pressures to conform to the surrounding culture are extremely high, especially in the middle school years. Be sure to affirm your young person's looks and personality strengths. Help them figure out what they are good at. Let them know they are accepted and totally valuable and always worth of love.

Girls often are especially worried about clothes and make-up. We let our girls begin wearing make-up at age 16, age 15 if they were not rebellious or giving us trouble. This is rather later than what I see currently with girls, but whatever you decide, make it a deliberate choice.

Be sure clothing choices are modest and appropriate. No cleavage should be showing. No lingerie straps hanging out. Teach them to stand in front of a mirror and see where attention is first drawn. Don't be afraid to say no to apparel that is too short, too tight, or too revealing. Our boys actually commented a time or two about some item their sisters might wear that made them uncomfortable or that drew inappropriate reactions from other boys.

Another positive way to help kids embrace being different is by allowing each of your children to have a different interest or hobby. If your family is large, it is

Intentional Parenting

tempting to lead our kids around as a group (or herd!). By not allowing them to all pick the same thing, each child could be good at something with no competition in the family.

Hormones

Preteen girls may deal with mood swings and emotions that intensify during that special time of month. I taught our girls that they would be dealing with this for many, many years to come, so they had to get a grip. Verbally shredding others or lashing out emotionally was not allowed. I told them I also had one day a month that I had to bite my tongue. Concerns women have at this time are valid, but they are exaggerated by the hormones. It's better to talk about things a week later when we are feeling more like ourselves.

For boys, this is a season of increasing hormones as well. Talk to them about appropriate thoughts and relationships with girls. Talk to them about the temptations of the internet and pornography. Beware of advertising with scantily clad models. There is so much in our culture that is accepted as normal, but the enemy uses it to set our young men up for trouble. Many a man who fights this battle as an adult began with a chance opportunity as a pre-teen.

Intentional Parenting

Pornography

Know your child's friends. Know what media and magazines are available in their homes. Have doors open when your children have friends over to visit. Do not let your children visit or play in homes you've not been in to see for yourself. Pay attention to what your kids are doing on the computer. You may need to have it in the family room where you can keep an eye on things.

Talking About Sex

If you don't, others will. As awkward as you may feel, you have to tackle this. Talk about the mechanics of biology and scriptural values within marriage. Talk about purity – in mind, body and soul. Follow up from time to time. Dad should ask boys, "How's your thought life?" Mom should ask girls, "What are you thinking about boys?" Lots of open communication (without trying to "fix" everything) will build relationships with your teens. Within marriage, sex is a gift from the Lord.

Sex Education in School

If your teen attends public school, you need to know what is being taught there regarding sex education. Usually this is taught in fifth grade and eighth grade. (Check this out on your state department of education's website. Public schools usually follow the "pragmatic" approach to sexuality – teens will be active anyway, so let's teach them about "safe" sex.) They may practice putting condoms on zucchini. And it may include teaching many unbiblical concepts such as lesbianism, being gay, bisexuality and transgender behavior (LGBT) as normal. (See Romans 1) The Bible teaches this as sinful and perverse. Our culture says it's genetic. And heaven forbid that we teach any values that might restrict or condemn anyone's personal choices. This lifestyle is unhealthy, dangerous, and often leads to an early death. You can preview sex ed curriculum and content used by your school. You can remove your student from classes you find objectionable. Be aware and proactive.

Your school may also advise your teen about an abortion without your knowledge. Start by being tuned in to your child and their friends. Be available to talk about even difficult things. Teach your children about right and wrong.

I believe sex ed should be abstinence-based and should have values incorporated. We are not dogs in heat. We are not simply animals who are unaffected by these biological matters. We are emotional and relational beings.

The wounded hearts and lasting damage of love affairs at too young an age is a high price to pay. Sexually transmitted diseases are at an all-time high for young people. These can ruin the future possibility of having children, and endanger their lives. Young people need guidance to avoid the pitfalls of unsafe relationships. They are in an emotionally fragile time of life. They should have an eye to lasting commitment, not fleeting one-night stands. Be the parent. Teach them.

And, by the way, your local school board should have a policy on movies shown in the classroom. Your student should not be able to view an R- rated movie without your permission. If this is not the case, contact your local school board. Take an evening and attend a meeting. Fight for your rights as a parent!

One of the stickier questions in our day is whether masturbation is okay or not. With all the sexual addiction in our society, this seems like a lightweight concern. My husband has counseled a number of people whose problems began with self-sex. Now they are trapped and trying to get out of all kinds of other sexual addictions. You can read his paper at www.renewalcs.org. Beware of friends spending the night and sharing this tantalizing information with your child.

Curfews

Curfews are a wonderful thing. Ours for our teens was 11 PM on school nights and 1 AM on weekends. Bars in our state close at 2 AM. I did not want my teenagers out on the road at the time when people who are intoxicated are out on the roads in force. Once when we were driving back into Colorado Springs at about 3 AM after a vacation, we were confronted by a large black pickup coming up the off-ramp going the wrong way onto the wrong side of the freeway. I honked and honked. And I yelled at the kids, "That's why I don't want you on the roads at this time of the morning!"

We asked our teens to give us a call and let us know where they were when they were out and about. We were not fearful and we trusted them. We felt it was a courtesy. We did the same and let them know where we, the parents, were and when we were on the way home if it was late.

Even when our adult daughter moved back in with us, we kept the curfew in place. At first she argued a bit, but later she thanked us when it gave her an excuse to leave a place she didn't want be. Of course exceptions can be made for special out-of-town events.

Intentional Parenting

Dating or Courtship?

There is so much pressure in the media, especially in TV and movies geared to teens, to have boyfriends or girlfriends and develop relationships too young. The message is that if you aren't in a dating relationship, there's something wrong with you. TV shows depict teenagers as independent and adults as absent.

I am amazed at parents who let their children begin dating at 12. Are you kidding?! Are they ready to choose mates for life? Are they mature enough to understand how not to be manipulated in relationships? Are they mature enough to deal with pressures and temptations that could lead to heartbreak or pregnancy? Absolutely not! Are they ready to start giving away pieces of their hearts to one boyfriend or girlfriend after another? Do you want to train them to always be shopping around, to have no self-worth unless they have a boyfriend or girlfriend? No wonder so many young people start adulthood emotionally broken and needy!

Song of Solomon 8:9 depicts the choice parents have with how they deal with their teen daughters. It says if a young girl is a "door", meaning open to flirtation, or we would say boy-crazy, the family will build a wall around her. They will put firm limits on her activities and how much freedom she has. If she is a "wall", not open to flirtation, not wanting to gad about or chase boys, they would set a garland (praise) on her. Today's parents can make a similar choice, based on how trustworthy a girl is. And we'd better know where our boys are and whom they are with.

    The biggest differences between dating and courtship is attitude. Most people see dating is shopping around, like trying on shoes. Unfortunately, in our culture, this can include sexual relationships before trust is earned and friendship is built. There is the constant fear of not being accepted, not being liked, and being rejected. Some young people are desperate to be wanted and accepted, so they become very serious in a very short time in relationships. This is not healthy.

    Courtship is more focused on finding a mate for life. You don't go out with someone you would not consider marriage material. Times together tend to be chaperoned or occur within family context. Usually a potential date begins with asking the father of the girl if they can go out. Boys who won't address this high bar are not considered worthy of consideration.

    Courtship has a weakness when there is forced exclusivity in friendships prematurely. I have known young

people who make a permanent choice too soon or too young, without getting to know very many other young people.
They may not know really know the qualities they are looking for in a future spouse. They may make a quick decision because there are no other choices available at the time.

    Perhaps group dating is a good possibility in between. There needs to be a setting in which young people can make friends, compare and decide what they want in a mate, and have a chance to meet people without getting serious. If your teenager can learn how to be a friend, how to work through relational problems, how to understand different personalities, how to be true to themselves and their values, they will be miles ahead. **These things are the foundation for a good marriage.** I repeat: relationships that skip this step (often moving on to physical involvement) never have the foundation laid properly for a lasting marriage. I guarantee you that they will have big problems within a few years, often with trust issues.

    Later in this chapter I'll give you a list of my favorite resources for when your young person is ready for Dating, Courtship and Marriage.

Intentional Parenting

Satan's Lies

Satan will tell your child that they are ugly, that people don't like them or approve of them, that you don't really love them and so on. He will tell them they need to look a certain way or act a certain way to be liked or loved. Isaiah 45:9 was a shock to me in my early 20's. It says the pot cannot say to the potter, "Why have you made me like this?!" (My paraphrase) My dislike of certain of my features was like saying to God, "You didn't know what you were doing when you made me this way."

You need to catch these things and confront them. I have talked to young 20-something prodigals who have believed that everyone in the church judged them and didn't like them. It wasn't true. I surely hadn't thought that way or heard anyone else do so. Frankly, most people probably didn't think about them much at all.

Teach your teens (and young children) that love and success is not about performance or about looks. It's about finding your God-given talents and developing them fully. It's about using what you know and who you are to build the kingdom of God.

Only a very small percentage of women look like models. And what is valued by culture changes from time to

Intentional Parenting

time. Frankly, I think a lot of it has to do with what the "rich and famous" can afford. In centuries gone by, only the wealthy could afford to eat well. Being skinny was identified with being poor. Now, the wealthy can have plastic surgery and go to spas and do special dieting, so being "thin" is in. We must embrace our Creator's design and work to be as healthy as possible without being preoccupied with it or spending too many hours on it.

What about those who are not academically inclined? If that is the only way to be successful in your family, how will the non-academic child win? How will they define success? Again, focus on natural gifts and talents and what place those have in the kingdom of God.

Transitioning to Adulthood

Keep in mind the line-graph (page 135) and charts from chapter 17. You want your child to be capable of taking care of themselves and their business by the time they leave home. There is a healthy in-between mode for parents, just like raising plants in a greenhouse. You know they cannot stay in your greenhouse forever. At the proper time, you develop a plan and a schedule for setting the plants outside a bit at a time, getting it ready for cool nights ahead. The goal is for

Intentional Parenting

the plant to be in its own area, its own soil, and to grow to maturity and fruitfulness at the proper time.

So consider, how can you begin to let go? What kinds of things can you begin to shift over to your teenager? Whether it's buying their own toiletries or making dinner from start to finish once a week, you have to start somewhere. Here are some things we chose as part of the passing of responsibility (a.k.a. "letting go"):

- Age 12 or 13 – allowed to babysit (after some training) or do yard work as a job. Encouraged to tithe and save. Discussed subsequent spending and whether their choices were wise.
- Age 14 or 15 – As they became pickier about what shampoo, conditioner and toiletries they used, I felt it was a good time for them to buy what they wanted with their own money.
- Age 15 ½ - get own laundry hamper. Do own laundry separately from everyone else in family. Buying some clothes with their own money. See Chapter 17 notes on doing laundry.
- Age 16 – wearing make-up. (Age 15 if they are not being rebellious or difficult.) Teach them how to wear it appropriately for their features and certain

events. There are lots of resources online with which you can consult.
- Age 16 – learning to drive, with the provision that they would pay their share of car insurance on our policy. We provided and older car and took care of maintenance and tires. They had to buy own gas. If they had an accident or got a ticket, they would also pay for the increase in insurance. Several of the kids decided to wait on driving until 17 and 18. They said it wasn't worth it.
- Older teens and adult kids – cooking dinner for everyone in the family at least one night per week. If they let me know the ingredients they needed in advance, I made sure they were added to the grocery list.

Another way we prepared our kids for adult life was by easing them socially into "real life" about the time they were juniors in high school. We had homeschooled through most of their academic years. We chose homeschooling in order to provide more rigorous academics and less focus on socializing. But we knew that they needed to be prepared for what it was really like out there. One step was to have them take 2 classes at the local public high school (one child took a class at the community college) during their junior and senior years. I required foreign language (which we had not successfully addressed through homeschooling) and keyboarding (touch-typing). They could pick something else if they wanted. This gave our kids a chance to see that not everyone was like us, and learn to work to get along with them. It gave us many opportunities to talk about the choices others make and how those were not wise or productive. It showed them that the priorities of most people in our culture were very shallow and short-term. They also learned that not all learning was efficient like homeschooling. All this was happening while we were there to oversee it and discuss it with them. Don't wait until your kids are about to leave for college or the work world to have these kinds of talks.

    Several of our kids participated in short-term mission trips in their late teens and early 20's. This was a great experience for them, and they stayed in touch with their friends from these events for many years. One went to the Philippines through Teen Mania, another to Belarus with a college group. One of our daughters worked with a ministry to street people and addicts in another state. I've found that kids who see third-world countries and people in dire situations tend to be more thankful and have a clearer perspective on life and possessions.

After high school graduation, we told our kids that by fall they either needed to be enrolled in college, or they could pay us rent. This wasn't so we could make money, but it was to motivate them into making good choices. Rent was $150 per month (in the 90s). That helped pay for groceries and utilities, but most of all, it gave them more responsibility. When one of our daughters was getting married, she asked if she could move home (she shared an apartment with several girls) and apply her funds instead to the wedding costs. That was a smart choice we supported!

The goal is always moving them toward self-sufficiency and living an active and practical Christian faith. It's not about proving you know more or that they aren't ready to do things on their own. By allowing them personal strength and responsibility and by keeping communication flowing, we allowed and encouraged our goals to come to fruition in their lives. They became strong, thoughtful adults.

Talk, Talk, Talk

Parents must convey their wisdom and their moral convictions to their children. It is not the church's job, or the

Intentional Parenting

Sunday School teacher's job, or the Youth Pastor's job. It is your job. Know what you believe and why you believe it. Look up Bible verses that explain moral reasoning for dealing with everyday situations. Talk to your kids when you are driving, when you are watching TV, after you go to a movie or shopping. Tell the how God feels about current events. Affirm them when they are right. Adjust carefully and graciously when they are wrong. Be as careful with your teens as you would be with a co-worker at your job. Treat them with <u>utmost</u> <u>respect</u>.

Teach them to think analytically. Be careful not to impute your personal preferences as a moral doctrine. If you are athletic, but your child is not interested in sports, you cannot make that into a doctrine. This will only cause conflict and resentment. It is smart on your part to delineate between God's laws and your preferences.

Teach them what it means to match the talk to the behavior. Integrity means that the person is consistent through and through. What they say is what they live.

Teach them how to listen beyond what people say. This is the other half of talking that so many people miss. Teach them that new acquaintances have more to them than meets the eye.

Intentional Parenting

How to be a Good Listener as a Parent

Communication is one of the majorly important areas for dealing with teens. If you *really* listen, your kids will tell you what is in their hearts. You need to know what they are thinking. You want to be a part of the processing they go through with life's events. You need to be available as a sounding board. But if you aren't known as one who listens, this won't happen.

Communication with your teen is not about "winning" an argument or being right. It's about your child letting you into his or her world.

Here are some ways to make sure you are really listening to your child (or your spouse, for that matter!)

- Set aside distractions and busyness.
- Focus your attention – don't just pretend to listen or listen with half an ear. Don't daydream or let your mind wander while they are speaking.
- Give your child respect while listening. Let them finish what they have to say without interrupting. When they are finished, ask for clarification if you need it.
- Don't get side-tracked by details. Listen for the overall picture. Hear their heart.

- Don't mentally criticize or take apart what they are saying while they are speaking.
- Don't let inaccurate wording or charged expressions keep you from hearing their message.
- Be careful of your voice tone. You can say the right thing, but if your tone is sarcastic or angry, the message will come across differently.
- Be conscious of body language. Someone whose arms are crossed, whose face is set like stone, or who rolls their eyes is not really being a good listener.
- Avoid using phrases like, "You always…" or "You never…" These leave no room for improvement or even small amounts of success.
- Determine what the felt need and real need(s) are. Do they just want to be heard? Are they crying out for justice? Are they afraid and coming to you for protection? Are they trying to manipulate your feelings? Listen beyond the words.
- If they just want to be heard, don't try to "fix" everything. It is tempting to use these times to "rearrange their furniture" – to try to make them

Intentional Parenting

change. If you do this, don't be surprised if they don't come to you in the future.

- Don't plan what you are going to say while they are talking. This takes you away from listening well. It also causes you to focus on yourself rather than them.
- Don't jump to conclusions. Give them time and interest while they tell the whole story. Make sure you get both sides of the story before you make judgments.
- Don't get emotionally revved up about the topic. Listen calmly. If matters are upsetting, say you need time to think before you give a response. Take that time, whether it is a couple of hours or a day.
- Don't say things you don't mean in order to force a response from them. Being overly dramatic or threatening to withhold your love will not give you the results you want. Scripture says, "The anger of man does not work the righteousness of God." You can't plant weeds and reap strawberries.
- Do not feel compelled to have all the answers. If you don't know what an answer should be, say so. Tell them you will get more info and get back to them.

- If opinions differ, agree to disagree. When it comes to style, preferences, and tastes you can disagree without being disagreeable. Yet, be aware of the "non-negotiables." Truth is absolute. Spiritual principles don't bend to human thinking.

Fad or Danger?

When it comes to letting teens be responsible for their own actions, there are principles that drive what you allow. Here are some examples:

- Clothing – Within the limits of what you can afford, you provide the best you can. (See clothing lists in Appendix 3.) Even if your kids are buying their own clothes, you should still mandate that, whatever the style, all items must be modest and appropriate as discussed previously. Talk about how clothing sends a message – in business and in relationships. Our teens can be cool and fashionable without being provocative.

    Fads like tattoos were off-limits because they were symbols of rebellion. After they left home, it was up to them. Honestly, many clothing fads are vulgar and sexualized. Don't be afraid to enforce your family standards, but be sure they are based on principle, not personal style. I grew up in a family that did not believe girls should wear pants or make-up. Because I could not find those restrictions in scripture, I rejected them in my late teen and early adult years. Thankfully I did not reject my faith in the process.

- Music choices – We did some music appreciation courses, visiting the symphony and listening to many kinds of music. Our five children have greatly varied tastes, from country to opera to Christian pop. One even likes Christian heavy metal. We checked the lyrics on the songs they wanted to listen to. If the words encouraged sinful activities (like affairs or premarital sex) or were demeaning to others, that music was off-limits, even if they had to throw something in the trash. A time or two of losing the money that had cost them let them know I meant business. I challenged the content on secular radio stations, making them change the channel if the lyrics were inappropriate. We found that good (or bad) music really affected their attitudes and behavior.

And with so many different sounds in the house (I was in the middle), they had to close doors or wear headphones.

- Media and movie choices – We had a "no R-rated movies" rule in general. When it came to PG-13's, we checked content. (Focus on the Family's "Plugged In" is great for this.) We taught the kids to be discerning and choosy. If you are visual or auditory, things stick in your head. Be careful what you allow. Movies or TV that violate our moral principles will weaken our resolve to live by them. As much as I love to read, I've had to put a few very good authors on my "off-limits" list because their content has become too explicit. Even seemingly innocent children's movies can have witches (condemned in scripture) and new age religious teachings. Movies and TV have "normalized" sinful behavior and desensitized our culture more and more over the last two generations. Restrictions on sexuality and horrible language have been removed. You must be the filter. Don't be afraid to stop the DVD or walk out of the theater if you must. You set the standards for your family and enforce them, no matter what others are doing or allowing.

- Participating with family activities – I've seen families allow teens to stay home from family vacations or choose not to participate in family events. I don't think that is healthy. If the teen has to work, I can understand it, but if possible try to make the schedules work to be together.
- Church attendance together is good, but after they are of age or have finished high school, let them choose. Don't enforce attendance for the sake of appearances. In their early adult years some of our kids attended different churches than we did, even though they still lived at home. We had taught them enough spiritual truth and had discussed it thoroughly. We trusted them to make quality, thoughtful decisions. We were glad they were going to healthy churches and growing in the Lord. Our parenting was not about marching in lock-step.
- Attitudes – Remember that what you allow is what you are training into your young person. Rolling their eyes, sighing and saying, "Whatever!" are not acceptable behaviors. Respect is a requirement.

Controlled tones are mandated. Yelling is not allowed. I once told my teenage boys that they would have to respect me even when *they* were 55 years old! They were aghast, but I assured them it was so.

If you are having frequent attitude problems with your teenager, have a sit-down meeting and dig deeper to find out why. If they are not just trying to be "big stuff", find out if there are deeper issues going on inside their hearts. Are they frustrated with you because they feel you are too controlling? Are they being influenced by bad friends? Are they hurt because you haven't kept your word about something? Talk it through. Do all you can to maintain a healthy relationship with them. (Reminder: this does not equal being their buddy. That comes later, after they leave home and probably after they are over 21.)

Choosing Healthy Friends

In our attempts to win others to Christ, we may be tempted to compromise when it comes to friendships. This is unwise. We will have many acquaintances in life, but close friends have a huge influence on us. I had acquaintances who wanted my kids to spend time with their kids so that my kids' good qualities would rub off on theirs. First of all, that's the parent's job, not my kids' obligation. And it really doesn't work.

There are kids with whom I had to limit the amount of time my kids could spend with them. And some that I hung around a lot if they were there. Once, I took a neighbor's child by the hand and took them home to their mother. I explained her child was not welcome at my house until he could behave. (He was swearing and hitting.) Don't be afraid to uphold your family standards with guests.

Also, there are kids who are bad combinations together. Individually, they are okay, but with that one young person, they always push each other into trouble. It's like gun powder and nitroglycerin. Together they make dynamite.

Bullying

Bullying has become such a hot topic, and is sometimes tied to teen suicide. In one case in our city, the teen had asked all the adults in his life for help with being bullied and nothing changed. He finally gave up and ended his life. Tragic!

Because parents today are so busy, one parenting article I read recently talked about teaching kids to "self-advocate". This meant the child must learn to go to talk to school officials or teachers, asking for assistance with problems. This made me angry. Where are the adults? At work? At the gym? While this is a good skill for kids to learn, your child had better know that you are right behind them if they don't get action. Be committed enough to your child to take off work if necessary to see that their needs are met, no matter how busy you are or how tough your job is.

If school actions are not sufficient, be prepared to contact the police or pull your child out of that school to protect them. Your child should never feel hopeless that adults just don't care enough to help them.

What about Youth Groups?

Because you are FOR your teen, you will want to check out the youth group they might attend and what goes on there. Make sure the leaders are healthy examples in their faith, not just adults who still act like teenagers. What is the purpose of the group? What is the focus? Is there a good mix of kids coming to Christ and those who are established in their faith or is the whole group a bunch of rebels being contained? Is there good supervision for all activities? Is your child emotionally ready for this kind of group? Is there a good balance of Bible studies and fun activities? Are the majority of the kids serious about their faith?

Heads-up: there are unbelievers, even predators, who see church as a good place to find nice, innocent teens to ensnare. Some like the challenge. Some want a "good girl," but have no intention of being a good man. Even those who are new Christians need time to prove up in their faith – to show fruit, to show it will last. Don't feel bad for saying no to relationships or activities you feel uncomfortable with. Time will tell, and you will see whether that person is for real later on.

Spiritual Choices
Covered in Chapter 18, Spiritual Life.

Teen Rebellion
Dr. Tim Kimmel wrote the book, literally, on *Why Christian Kids Rebel.* He addresses some of the events that can trigger teen rebellion and some of the parental inconsistencies that feed teen rebellion. Perhaps reading it before you have teenagers should be required as a form of inoculation for parents.

Parenting our kids during these difficult seasons is so hard. Do not give up. Failure is not an option. Continue to show and speak your love. Be consistent with discipline and requirements.

When kids choose to be rebellious, your love must be with a toughness that allows them to experience consequences. You cannot cut in and take over and remove consequences that their actions have earned. This is where your past history as a parent, with not threatening but following through will be helpful. Your child will already know you mean business.

You cannot allow a child to bring illegal substances into your home or influence younger children with risky behaviors. Dr. Dobson's book *Love Must Be Tough* spawned "Tough Love" groups where parents could discuss these situations and find mutual support in seeing kids through these things. Even if kids try to manipulate you and make you feel bad, you must stick to your guns throughout the process.

Teen Suicide

Teen suicide has become all too common. For some it may seem like the only way to end the emotional pain they are experiencing. Teach your children that this is wrong. It violates the sixth commandment. It is a permanent solution to a temporary problem. The lack of respect for life in our country is growing every day. Talk about suicide and a choice and tell your child, "Don't you DARE leave me like that! Don't you leave me with that as the last memory of you!" Be watchful if your child has unresolved problems or depression. Talk to them about getting help if a friend is talking about suicide. Call 911 and get intervention for *anyone* who is threatening suicide. They can be evaluated in a lock-down setting for 48 to 72 hours and get the help they need. Check out the Mayo Clinic's online articles describing symptoms that are warning signs for suicide.

Setting the Course for the Future
All too soon, you will be facing helping your teen make decisions for life direction. Frankly, this was the scariest, hardest time for me in all of parenting. I remember asking God if we could just go back to potty-training at this point. Choosing life mates, deciding on careers, setting the course for the kind of person they wanted to be was huge! And I couldn't make them do what I wanted at this stage. They had to choose.

Hopefully you have paid attention to what he or she is good at and in what they are interested. One place to start is asking are they more inclined toward dealing with **data** or **people** or **things**. Some people like working with numbers and thrive on details and statistics. Others prefer a job with lots of people interaction. Or perhaps they would like to handle and organize products in an inventory. Would they hate working indoors and prefer an outdoor job? Or would they be happy with a job that requires sitting still in an office or cubicle?

Understanding these kinds of things, you can now look for ways to support your young person. Perhaps you can help them do volunteer service in an area that might connect them to future work. If you know people in a job or field they are considering, find out if that person would take your teen to work for a day and watch what they do. Can you find a tutor to help them deepen their knowledge or improve their skill set? Are there tutorials, disks or books that would assist in training? The Dictionary of Occupational Titles (available online) gives descriptions of thousands of jobs, and codes for the required education for those jobs.

If college is a part of their chosen direction, contact a few colleges that offer degree programs in that field, and find out what their entrance requirements are. Then work backwards to make sure you have the bases covered in time for college. By planning ahead, you can avoid paying for remedial classes, for which your child may not receive credit, at the beginning of college. Are there deadlines you must be aware of regarding applications and financial aid forms? It's quicker to find out from the college admissions department than to try to get details through high school counselors. Take time to explore the reference section of your local library. Ask about books there that are filled with college and scholarship information. If your child's field of interest is not academic, consider how you can find resources to connect them to growth and learning in that field.

Consider "the trades" such as electricians, tile laying, brick and masonry, and so on. Many businesses send their workers to training for the specific skills needed in that industry. We know several young men who are making very good money in HVAC (Heating, Ventilation, and Air Conditioning) and in the oil and gas industry, for example. They've been trained on things like computer controls and driving a crane by their companies.

Then ask yourself, are there jobs available in this field? This may take some research, but there is no point in helping your child get a degree in sociology, only to have them work in a car rental place. The Bureau of Labor Statistics has a list of fastest growing occupations and what the pay level is for each.

For kids who are going to college, I highly recommend a class or a conference in Christian Worldview as described in the Spiritual Life chapter. Secular colleges require "humanities" classes which equals studies in humanism. There is huge pressure to conform to worldly and perhaps liberal thought. Even Christian colleges may or may not embrace the authority and truth of the Bible. Parents need to do their homework before sending their young people to college. Some professors have an agenda that undermines faith. In our society that emphasizes education beyond all else, there are many parents grieving over the changes in their children's attitudes toward Christianity due to the influences of the college years.

Preparing for Marriage

Having stated earlier that the first priority in finding a life-mate is friendship, here are a few more thoughts to guide you

Intentional Parenting

in guiding your teen in the areas of dating, courtship, and marriage.

Encourage group activities rather than pairing off. There is safety in numbers if the participants have good character and purpose. They will be able to have fun, and to see how their friends interact with others. They will learn who is trustworthy and who is catty, who is quick to anger, and who is domineering. Perhaps you can be the host of some of these events. We made sure our house was the place to hang out. We could listen to the talk from upstairs, and knew where the kids were and who they were with. Later, we had discussions about how others' behavior, how they spoke of their families, how they treated other people.

Teach teens what good communication looks like: *both* parties should be heard, both should be good listeners. They should be accepted for who they are, not morphed into a non-entity so the other person can feel good. Marriage relationships are not meant to "complete" or fix people who are half there or who loaded down with baggage and woundedness. If someone is in that position, they need time to heal before they are ready to commit to a long-term relationship. My sister says that relationships are not addition ($\frac{1}{2}$ person + $\frac{1}{2}$ person = 1 whole), but multiplication (1 whole person X 1 whole person = 1 couple). Both parties should be *whole* people, giving all their strengths to the relationship.

Teach them to have good personal boundaries. They don't have to go anywhere they don't want to or do anything they don't want to, just to be accepted. They have to live with themselves and any consequences after the fact. We told our kids they could always call us and we would come and get them at any time without condemnation for what others were doing being extended to them. Make it easy for your kids to do what is right. Make it easy for them to bail out of a bad situation. Consider the book *Boundaries in Dating* by Cloud and Townsend.

Find out what the current dating terminology means. One of our children requested permission to "date" a young man. We said okay, then later found out that rather than going out occasionally, it now meant the same thing as "going steady" did in our day. Yikes! We didn't know what we had agreed to!

Don't be afraid to speak up when you are uncomfortable with a person or an activity. We pressured ourselves to be accepting and kind toward a person one of our children married. He turned out to be abusive and controlling. It was a long time and much agony before our daughter escaped to a safe house. It took years to rebuild her life.

Help your teens identify qualities they like and prefer in a future mate. I remember identifying the trait of gentleness in a guy I knew in high school. We never dated, but it was something I watched for in men, and noticed later in the wonderful man I married. After 37 years, it's still one of my favorite qualities of all his great ones.

When your young person is really considering the person they think they want to marry, get them the book *101 Questions to Ask Before You Get Engaged*. It is filled with topics they can discuss about their family backgrounds, their philosophies about raising children, their life goals, and more. Remind them they are choosing a life-partner, not just someone to make them feel good about themselves. They must be able to work together, play together, pray together, and trust each other with their finances and their emotional safety. Pre-engagement counseling is even better than pre-marital counseling. Even if they get engaged, tell them you are FINE with breaking the engagement if they feel they have made a mistake. Better to cancel the invitations than live a miserable existence for many years. (Reminder: You are FOR them!)

With several of our children, I prayed fervently that they would REALLY get to know that person. I knew that doing so would either draw them closer to one another, or drive them apart by seeing what they did not want to live with. Those prayers were answered again and again as they took time to discover what that person was made of. I also prayed for some people they were interested in to move away or be transferred out of town. That happened as well. A mama's prayers work!

For premarital counseling, see what your church offers. If that is not available, consider the following:
- *Before You Say I Do* – a workbook to do together
- *Marriage on the Rock* – a DVD series on marriage
- *Financial Peace University* (Dave Ramsey)

We also asked our kids who were getting engaged to wait at least 6 months while they went through these resources. We did not expect them to change their minds, but we did think they would have a stronger start with these under their belts. They were much better prepared to face life's difficulties with these tools in their tool box.

Living together before marriage (co-habitation) is so common in our culture. It is wrong according to the Bible. Pre-marital sex is a sin. It also undermines the trust in a relationship. Statistically, couples who live together before marriage are 1 ½ times more likely to divorce than couples who do not live together prior to marriage. (And only 50% of *those* make it.) Prior to marriage, a girl is still in a position to negotiate for what she wants in a relationship. A boy pursues (as he should), but she gets to choose whether or not to say yes. After a couple lives together, the deal is signed. If she thinks she can go back and renegotiate, he will point to the living arrangement, and say everything is fine. She has already closed the deal by giving herself physically.

Finally

No matter how hard you try, you won't do everything perfectly as a parent. The teen years can be a joy or a trial. They will be the culmination of all you have invested in your child. By being intentional as a parent, you can be sure that, as much as it depends on you, your child has had the right input to give them every opportunity to make right choices for their adult lives.

Intentional Parenting

No matter what they choose, you keep loving. You choose your words wisely. You keep on being FOR them. And you pray they learn any tough lessons sooner rather than later, going down a long tough road.

Endnotes

Truetolerance.org is a website for parents that reviews and discusses sex ed curriculum. **Focus on the Family**
James 2:9-10
1 Corinthians 15:33
Love Must Be Tough / Straight Talk by Dr. James Dobson
Consider Summit Ministries or The Truth Project… in order to solidify your student's Christian Worldview before college.
Boundaries and *Boundaries in Dating* by Cloud and Townsend
101 Questions to Ask Before You Get Engaged by H. Norman Wright
Before You Say I Do by H. Norman Wright and Wes Roberts – a workbook to do together
Marriage on the Rock by Jimmie Evans – a DVD or CD series on marriage
Financial Peace University by Dave Ramsey
Made to Shine, A Girls Only Devotional by Becca Leander Nicholson and Elissa Leander Tipps – The Sonflowerz www.Sonflowerz.com

Chapter 20
Adult Children & Prodigals

Our adult children want desperately for us to accept that they are adults, that they know what they are doing, and that they are capable of making decisions. At the same time, we know their strengths and weaknesses. It is so tempting to push to continue in the role as parent advisor/corrector. This often causes resentment and unnecessary strife. After all, we have trained them to be self-sufficient adults, have we not?

After raising our children to be pretty much like us (if we do a good job), you will find they make the greatest of lasting friends. They may discover you were amazingly smart about life when they hit 22 or 23, and remember what an amazing job you did when they start having kids of their own. (Remember all those times I said you are not their buddy? NOW you get to be one.)

Here are some guidelines to help you relate to your adult children (specifically those for whom you are no longer providing financial support).

- Continue that posture that you are FOR them.
- Stay in touch frequently.

Intentional Parenting

- Be supportive and encouraging with your words. Make it easy for them to want to talk to you.
- Wait to be asked for advice.
- Be scriptural with your advice. Life is not about doing what makes them happy, but about doing what is right in God's eyes.
- Support their marriages and career choices. Love and accept their spouses. (A friend once told us his mother never thought anyone was good enough for her sons. She made a terrible mother-in-law.)
- Give them room to grow, even to make mistakes. You want the same, right?
- Continue to ask them what they are learning spiritually, what God is speaking to them personally.

Boomerang Kids

If they are still living with you, or have come back to live with you, you need house rules that apply to everyone (even you).

- Discuss a mindset of teamwork in the home.
- How will they help financially? We required our adult children who lived with us (one for a short time, while they saved up for a home, one for eight years as

a single mom) to pay rent. This was to help with groceries and utilities. It was a discipline for them. Whether we needed the money or not was not the point, it was good for them to bear their adult responsibilities.

- How will they help with housework? We divided some of the responsibilities, such as cooking for the entire household on two to three nights per week, which days they could use the washer and dryer, and who would clean what areas. Of course they were required to keep their own spaces clean. Shared spaces meant shared cleaning. We planned meals together, then I shopped for all the food.
- What are the boundaries for grandchildren? We defined rooms that were off-limits to kids or off-limits to toys. We set priorities with TV use. We were clear about what snacks were always available (fruit and granola bars), and what food required permission first. (Things marked with a black X were ingredients for planned meals.)
- Be respectful of their privacy and their spaces.
- Our curfew was still in effect. (See Chapter 19.) I did not want to support them, only to make it easy for

them to stay out late and live a wild life. This also gave them an excuse to leave places where things were getting uncomfortable. Out of respect for each other, my husband and I also gave them a call when we would be later than planned.

- We were not built in babysitters. We would babysit occasionally, but their children were their responsibility. They had to find and pay for babysitters.
- We did not correct their children unless they were not home. We referred problems to them to take care of. We tried to be silent about discipline matters, waiting to be asked for advice. Parents know what they are working on. Grandparents may not know the whole story. And again, it's their job.
- We did not get up in the night with their babies or clean up their children's messes. These were their responsibilities.
- We preferred they attend church (not necessarily ours), but did not mandate that. Our conversations were about their hearts, not just their actions. We did ask the "How are you doing spiritually?" type questions from time to time.

- Do not allow anything to go on in your home that violates your conscience. If they are living a lifestyle that offends you, you cannot host them in your home. This includes movies, drinking, friends and so on. And they cannot spend the night elsewhere, having an affair, and continue to be supported by you.

College Kids

For the kids whom you are supporting at college, try a blend of the above.

- Talk to them about what is going on – spiritually, in relationships, in classes. Remember you are FOR them. Don't have a suspicious tone, probing to see if they are messing up.
- Talk about the pressures they may be experiencing that may threaten their faith, their safety, or their values.
- Set reasonable boundaries about how they can use your money. Ask them if they have what they need (maybe not all they *want*). One family I know pays for room and board, but the student must pay tuition and college costs. This motivates them to get (and keep)

scholarships. It also encourages them to do well in classes and not have to retake them.

- Monitor grades and productivity. Require that they be faithful with what you are giving them.
- Be careful to affirm what is good. If you need to challenge them, do it by asking questions rather than making commands. Draw them out in an adult conversation.

Adults in Their Own Right

Recently I reviewed how much our five grown children needed me during the course of a busy week. One asked for advice about Facebook "drama" with a cousin, one called to talk and process a problem, one came over to borrow jewelry for a party, one went to the hospital to get his appendix out, and one needed help with a home improvement project. Granted, this was an unusual week, but I was so grateful to be a part of their lives!

I love having our kids and grandkids go camping with us or sharing family birthdays or attending their events like recitals or seeing them perform for worship dance. I treasure their friendship. They have been supportive when I was ill or going through a crisis. I have helped when they needed an extra pair of hands to do a wedding or an emergency babysitter while someone went to the emergency room. We treat each other with utmost respect.

Prodigals

There is no guarantee that your child will continue in the path on which you have started them. I wish I could say that if you follow the principles in this book or if you are careful to follow some other 10-step program, the chance of having a prodigal son or daughter does not exist. Our children have a choice. At some point, just like us, they make decisions and walk them out. Some people isolate their children trying to prevent rebellion. Some homeschool in order to protect their kids from outside influences. But no matter what plan you follow or what steps you take, they have a free will. They may choose whether to make wise or unwise choices, and even to endanger themselves and their children.

If you are dealing with a prodigal situation, you, too, have choices to make. How will you carry yourself? What will you say to this child? Will you let your pain and your anger separate you from this child? Will you turn inward and avoid contact? Will you protect yourself from connecting with them and their messy life?

Intentional Parenting

One of our children went through a painful time like this, and we all lived to see it turn around. She has given us permission to share her story in the hope that it will help someone else through a similar situation.

During this time, the Lord whispered in my heart, **"If you don't fight for her, who will?"** He made it clear that I needed to stand by her and pray for her and speak truth to her no matter what happened. To love a child through their wrong choices, you must pray, pray, pray, and be patient. You must set your heart to be a long-hauler. You cannot, CANNOT give up!

Our precious daughter, who had been through so much with other pain and loss in an abusive marriage, had been living with us as a single mom. After several years, she got tired of waiting for God's best. She began dating a guy who was an unbeliever. Soon she found she was pregnant. She decided she had to try to make the best of the situation. She believed the lies of the enemy, and moved in with him, in spite of the way we had raised her to believe this was absolutely wrong.

We walked out "tough love" with her. We did not welcome her live-in boyfriend into our home. She and her children were always welcome, but he was not, unless he was

Intentional Parenting

ready to apologize for the injury done to our family, for the offense against our values. We had to stand firm on what we would allow in our home. We also had a younger daughter still living at home to protect, and she was *very* uncomfortable with the situation.

We could not protect our prodigal from what other people thought. We did not hide her situation. Our friends knew the truth of what was going on. We asked them to pray, but not to gossip. She had to deal with the intense reactions of her siblings. They exchanged heated words, some quite hurtful.

We did not adjust our theology or our commitment to scriptural principles to make her or her boyfriend comfortable. The truth we taught our kids while they were growing up was lasting truth, the grid through which human actions and events must be evaluated. We did not say, "Well, it's too bad, but God understands." We remained rock-solid in our faith and our commitment to truth. I prayed that the hurtful opinions of others would not cause lasting damage that would keep her from coming back to the Lord.

One of the important things you must do during this kind of event is to continue to speak your prodigal child's love language. (See Chapter 5.) Whether that is giving small gifts or giving words of affirmation for whatever you can find to affirm, keep communicating your love. Don't let this turn into a power struggle between your will or desire for control and their choices. It is so tempting to withhold your love in the midst of your hurt. Don't do it. Don't give the enemy the ammunition to lie to your child and say you don't love them, or that your love is performance-based.

Even before the baby was born, the father deserted our daughter. He left her with a pile of bills and a difficult pregnancy. She was about to be evicted from their rented townhome. We felt letting her live on the streets was not an option God would be pleased with. We opened our arms for her to come home, not knowing if she would repent and return to her faith.

I had already embraced this little one as a member of our family. I told our daughter that God is the giver of life. I began to pray she would come to know Jesus at a young age, that she would fulfill her destiny in Christ. We would welcome this child and love her as much as the other grandchildren.

Over the many months that followed, I found much to disagree with in our daughter's thinking. Much of the time, I had to remain silent. **I affirmed and encouraged any**

small movement in the right direction. I affirmed truth when she spoke it. I did not lecture or try to correct her thinking. I prayed for her a lot and waited for the Holy Spirit to do the work in her heart. Bit by bit her thoughts and her heart turned back toward the Lord. After about a year and a half, she repented and apologized to her dad and me. She called each of her siblings and apologized. Their acceptance took some time, but it came.

In the meantime, she moved back into our home. We followed guidelines above. We did not buy her diapers and formula. We let her get up at night and be the parent. She had to take care of the children when they were sick. We made sure there was food in the fridge and the utilities were paid kept on. We provided stability and security for her and the girls. She still had to work through the consequences of her choices. She paid her own car insurance and expenses. She worked part-time and paid a babysitter. Several times we paid for repairs on her car, but she paid us back. Essentially, we treated her like an adult.

God is so good. Six years later, she met and married a wonderful Christian man who is a good father to her two older girls. Subsequently, they gave birth to twins, a boy and a girl! They are joyfully serving God and thanking Him every day for His grace!

    Whatever comes as you enjoy life with your adult children, keep communicating. Affirm their choices that lead to a blessed life. Embrace their strengths, root for their personal growth. Love their spouses and children. Continue to build the legacy.

Conclusion

Living a Blessed Life

Intentional Parenting is hard work. But for those who embrace it, the benefits are tremendous. By setting goals and being proactive about training your children, you set your family up for success. By waiting until later in life to be their buddy, you set your family up to enjoy one another in their adult years. You prepare the next generation to face the greater difficulties that we know are ahead in this fallen world. You lay the groundwork for a legacy that you and your successive generations will enjoy for years to come.

Appendix 1
How to Choose a Good Church

Doctrine – Do they teach and believe the Bible is the Word of God, that even though it was authored by many men over a number of centuries, it is cohesive and authoritative. (Example: Do they believe in the virgin birth?) Read their doctrinal statement.

Structure – How is the church governed? Is there good accountability with the finances? What recourse is there if leaders commit gross sin? (Example: If a pastor commits adultery, who can remove him from leadership?)

Philosophy – What is most important in the identity of the church? Is all ministry done by those on staff, or do volunteers participate in the programs of the church? Is sin accepted as all right or are people challenged to grow?

Balance – Is there a good balance between evangelism, discipling new believers, challenging the growth of long-time believers? Or is the focus predominantly one or the other? Is there a good mix of various generations?

Growth – Is the church growing? Why yes, or why not?

Missions – Is the church involved in missions, both in the U.S. and abroad? Are there opportunities for youth and families to participate in short term mission projects?

Ministry to the poor, especially "widows and orphans" – God places a high priority on this. What does this church do?

Intentional Parenting

Programs – Does the church offer programs for each of your children? Are the programs Biblically-based and strong? (See Chapter 19 on teens and youth group section.)

Pastoral Care – What are your expectations about connecting with the senior pastor? Is the size of the church conducive to that? What kind of pastoral care do they engage in? (Hospital visitation, a call to see how you are if you've been sick or absent... This may not be a realistic expectation if the church is large.)

Style – The way the singing and music function, the speaking or teaching style of the pastor, and so on. Décor, lighting, and so many other details may make you comfortable or uncomfortable. This is usually what people notice first, although it is not the most substantive issue on which to base a decision of whether this is the right church for you or not.

Appendix 2
A-B-C List of Scriptures to Memorize

Children are best at memorizing in the elementary grades. Do not leave them out of this activity! (New International Version – NIV unless otherwise stated.)

A – For all have sinned and fall short of the glory of God. Ro. 3:23
B – That if you confess with your mouth, "Jesus is Lord, "and believe in your heart that God raised him from the dead, you will be saved. Ro. 10:9
C – Children, obey your parents in the Lord, for this is right. Eph. 6:1
D – Here I am! I stand at the door and knock. If anyone hears my voice and opens the door, I will come in and eat with him, and he with me. Rev. 3:20
E – The eyes of the Lord range throughout the earth to strengthen those whose hearts are fully committed to him. 2 Chron. 16:9
F – For it is by grace you have been saved, through faith – and this is not from yourselves, it is the gift of God – not by works so that no one can boast. Eph. 2:8,9
G – ...the one who is in you is greater than the one who is in the world. 1 John 4:4
H – Anyone who claims to be in the light but hates his brother is still in the darkness. 1 John 2:9
I – If I had cherished sin in my heart, the Lord would not have listened. PS. 66:18 (KJV – If I regard iniquity in my heart, the Lord will not hear me.)
J – Jesus answered, I am the way and the truth and the life. No one comes to the Father except through me. John 14:6
K – But seek first his kingdom and his righteousness, and

all these things will be given to you as well. Matt. 6:33

L – Greater love has no one than this, that he lay down his life for his friends. John 15:13

M – …if you have faith as small as a mustard seed, you can say to this mountain, 'Move from here to there' and it will move. Nothing will be impossible for you. Matt. 17:20

N – No one can serve two masters. Either he will hate the one and love the other, or he will be devoted to the one and despise the other. You cannot serve both God and Money. Matt. 6:24

O – Be not overcome with evil, but overcome evil with good. (KJV) Ro. 12:17

P – I press on toward the goal to win the prize for which God has called me heavenward in Christ Jesus. Phil. 3:14

Q – Do not quench the Holy Spirit. 1 Thes. 5:19 (Amp)

R – Resist the devil, and he will flee from you. James 4:7

S – You may be sure that your sin will find you out. Num. 32:23

T – In this world you will have trouble. But take heart! I have overcome the world. John 16:33

U – And the peace of God, which transcends all understanding, will guard your hearts and minds in Christ Jesus. Phil 4:7

V – (Vengeance) Do not take revenge, my friends, but leave room for God's wrath, for it is written: "It is mine to avenge; I will repay, says the Lord. Ro. 12:19

W – For we are God's workmanship, created in Christ Jesus to do good works, which God has prepared in advance for us to do. Eph. 2:10

X – I want you to be wise (excellent – KJV) about what is good, and innocent about what is evil. Ro. 16:19

Y – Don't let anyone look down on you because you are young, but set an example for the believers in speech, in life, in love, in faith and in purity. 1 Tim. 4:12

Z – Never be lacking in zeal, but keep your spiritual fervor, serving the Lord. Ro. 12:11

Others:
John 3:16-17
Romans 6:23
Romans 8:28
Romans 12:1
The Beatitudes Matt. 5:1-12
The Lord's Prayer Matt. 6:9-13 or Luke 11:2-4
Psalm 23
Fruit of Spirit Gal. 5:22-23
Phil. 4: 6 Be anxious for nothing, but in everything, with prayer and supplication make your requests known to God.
Phil. 4:13 I can do all things through Christ who gives me strength.
To obey is better than sacrifice. 1 Sam. 15:22

Scripture Songs

This was more popular during the 70s and 80s, but I have found it a good way to cause scripture to lodge in the heart and brain. CD's of such music are still available.

Intentional Parenting

Appendix 3
Sample Clothing List for Children

I began this list after reading about George Mueller who had orphanages in England during the 1800's. He set minimum provision standards and even required that his children have 3 pairs of shoes each, a generous provision in my mind for that era.

Adjust this to fit your family. You may need more items if you do not have your own washer and dryer handy. If your children live part-time with another parent, they will need clothing at both places, especially coats. (Otherwise you will find your provision for them "migrating" to the other house.)

If you are given "hand-me-downs", this list can help you sort through and pare down an over-abundance. (Especially if storage space is an issue.) If you have babies or toddlers who are not yet potty-trained, you know you'll need to increase the numbers (about double) because they go through clothes more frequently.

A word here also about shopping at thrift stores: unless you are buying designer brands, I have found that often an item from the thrift store at half-price is half worn out. Instead I decided to buy inexpensive items new from a

Intentional Parenting

discount store (like Target or Walmart). Often they have <u>very</u> good deals on their clearance racks. I wanted our kids to feel taken care of and to get to enjoy the "newness." They still had some hand-me-downs from older siblings and cousins, but I made sure they had some things new. Also, I do <u>not</u> allow used underwear or shoes.

Girls' List – Spring / Summer

Item	Should Have	Actual
Dresses	4	_____
Dressy Slacks	2	_____
Jeans	2	_____
Shorts	4	_____
Tops / Shirts	7-8	_____
Panties	8-10	_____
Bras (if older)	4	_____
Slips	to match dresses	_____
Socks	8-10	_____
Light-weight Pajamas	4	_____
Robe	1	_____
Swimsuit & Cover-up	1	_____
Jacket / Sweater	2	_____
Shade Hat	1	_____
Shoes – church	1	_____
Shoes – tennies	1	_____
Shoes – sandals / flip flops	1 or 2	_____

Girls' List – Fall / Winter
Similar to above, plus:

Tights	3	_____

Intentional Parenting

Wooly Sweaters / Sweatshirts	3-4	_____
Mittens or Gloves*	1	_____
Hat	1	_____
Snow Boots	1	_____

Boys' List – Spring / Summer

Item	Should Have	Actual
Dress Pants	2-3	_____
Jeans	4	_____
Shorts	4-6	_____
Dress Shirts	2	_____
Tops / Shirts	7-8	_____
Underwear	8-10	_____
Socks	8-10	_____
Light-weight Pajamas	4	_____
Robe	1	_____
Swimsuit & T-shirt	1	_____
Jacket / Sweater	2	_____
Shade Hat	1	_____
Shoes – church	1	_____
Shoes – tennies	1	_____
Shoes – sandals / flip flops	1 or 2	_____

Boys' List – Fall / Winter
Similar to above, plus:

Wooly Sweaters / Sweatshirts	3-4	_____
Mittens or Gloves*	1	_____
Hat	1	_____
Snow Boots	1	_____

*You may want to purchase extra mittens and gloves from the "Dollar Store" as they seem to disappear quite easily. I love the long crocheted strings that attach and hang out each coat sleeve.

Index

Abortion 130, 270
Academic goals 96
Acts of service 56
Abuse by siblings 56
Abusive parents, other see chapter 5; 46, 127
Adoption 79, 105
Adult children 305-306
    Returning (see Boomerang kids)
Affirmation 8, 14, 32, 57, 62, 104, 194, 314
Age of accountability 247
Aggression 168
A-H-E-N 83
Allowance 94
Analytical parent 41-42
Analytical thinking, kids 237, 249, 262, 282
Anger see chapter 8; 7, 30, 32, 33, 176, 216, 222, 285, 311
Anger, children's 85
Anger, hormonal 84
Angry words 85
Answered prayer 65, 107
Anxiety 221-222
Anxiety, testing 234
Apologizing to children 17, 18, 25, 30, 40, 55, 92, 155, 160
Apology, as part of correction 148, 149, 173, 212
Applying scripture 253
Arguing v. obedience 21, 40, 138-139, 169
Attending church 257-259, 289

Appendix 1
Authority of the Bible 13, 37, 43
Authority, Parental 13, 43, 69
Babysitting, teens 232, 278
Bad eating habits 201-203
Bad friends 183, 290
Bad language 175, 188
Balance in parenting 14, 101, 119, 204
Behavior, basic 91, 93
Behavior, public 92-93, 169-172
Behavior, with company 172-173
Behavior standard 35, 93-94, 95, 106
Bible stories 245
Blended families 77
Blessings 3, 11, 40, 60, 71, 129, 317
Boasting 203-204
Boredom 243
Boomerang kids 306
Borrowing 124
Boundaries 30, 40, 42, 44, 47, 80, 123, 172, 240, 300
Boy-crazy 273-274
Bribing 94
Bright children and obedience 137
Buddy parenting 6, 40-41, 366, 290, 305, 317
Bullying 39, 56, 168, 180, 291
Careers 235-237, 295-298
Celebrating success 53, 203, 204
Character goals 96, 108

Character trait list   112-114
Character resources   108-109
Character trait calendar   110-112
Character training   see chapter 11; 106-114
Cheating   173
Child-centered parenting   28-29, 189
Church attendance   254-256, 286
Church nursery   258-259
Clash of Wills   15, 158
Clothing List   180, Appendix 3
Clothing, modest and appropriate, teens   165, 232, 265, 267, 286
Co-habitation   43, 303
College   103, 280-281, 297-298, 309
College preparation   262, 298, 304, 309
Coming to faith, children   246
Coming to faith later in life   17-18
Communication, listening   180, 198-200, 269, 281, 283-286, 299
Complaining   161, 176-177, 200, 218
Conflict Resolution   41, 52, 63, 74, 84, 98, 199, 236, 282
Consequences   14, 33, 43-45, 82, 122, 130-131, 140, 144, 146, 151-156, 158, 174, 178, 191, 206, 212, 294, 200, 315
Consistency   11, 41, 74-75, 125, 139, 251
Consistency of requirements   25, 77, 89, 163, 294
Constructive Criticism   237
Contrarians   118-119
Control (by child)   28, 140, 160, 174
Control (muscle)   96
Control (of tongue)   85, 188, 189, 290
Control (self-)   29, 92, 133-135, 189, 218, 219, 225
Control (things you can't)   77, 249, 265, 290, 314
Control vs. Training chart   135
Cooking skills list   241-242
Correction   14, 16, 23, 32, 50, 104, 112, 122, 142-157, 194
Correction process (steps)   142-149
Counseling   47-48, 51, 64, 79, 80, 84, 223, 301, 302
Counting before discipline   20
Courtship   273-275, 299
Covetousness   184
Curfew   154, 272, 307
Cut-downs   53
Craft, Diane   141, 182
Critical thinking   249, 262
Criticism   54, 117, 194
Cruelty   176
Crying, Constant   87, 88, 161-162, 258
Curses   3
Cursing   175
Dating   273-275, 299, 300
Defeat, spiritual   107
Demeaning   32, 73, 127, 287
Deployed parents   78
Devotional habit   95, 107, 225, 248, 251-252
DiSC personality test   98-99,

105

Discontent 176-177, 195
Disrespect Chapter 12; 76, 91, 115-117, 122, 127
Dissatisfaction 176-177, 195
Distractions, spiritual 107, 283
Domestic violence 46-48
Double-Standard parenting 24
Driving, teens 154, 179, 236, 265, 279
Dyslexia 181
Emotional intelligence 101
Enabling parent 43-45
Engagement 301-304
Entitlement 44, 186
Envy 187, 192
Euthanasia 130
Evangelism 66, 318
Ex-spouses 74-76
Examples as adults 10, 18, 20, 50, 60, 62, 80, 85, 106, 110, 126, 156, 160, 184, 223, 250, 292
Extroverts 69, 98-99
Fads 286
Faith in children 65, 103, 160, 180, 245, 248, 292-293, 309
Family goals Chapter 9; 93-97, 108, 265
Family standard 41, 93, 139, 145, 287, 291
Favoritism 25
Fear-based parenting 16, 179-180, 221-222, 264, 265, 272
Fear of the Lord 13, 261
Fear of being different, teens 267
Fearfulness 179-180, 221-222, 265, 272

Feelings of others 208
Feminism 71-73
Fighting 47, 130, 180
First-time obedience 20-21
Focus, Lack of 57, 137, 150, 181, 283
Foolishness 15-16, 44, 140, 184, 245
Forgetfulness 144, 150, 182-183, 221
Forgiveness 55, 148, 214
Foster care 79, 207, 213
Friends, bad 122, 183, 266, 269-271, 290, 309
Friends, choosing 38-39, 95, 96, 103, 151, 183, 273-274, 298-299
Gambling 184
Gay 48, 270
Gift-giving 25, 56
Gifted Children Chapter 10; 100-103, 137
Goals, character 108-114
Goal in parenting 45
Goals, family 89-94
Goals for each child 95-97
Golden Rule 97, 120, 122
Gossip 184-185, 250
Grandparents, abusive 127
Grandparents' role 4, 18, 77-78, 116, 201, 261, 308
Grandparents, living with 77-78
Gratitude, Lack of 186
Greed 9, 187
Grumpiness 187-188
Guests and respect for property 123-124
Hard work of parenting 2, 12, 26, 88, 157, 167, 203, 239, 317

Harsh parent   32-33, 117
Harshness ("Kind words only")
     86-87
Hate   10, 76, 86, 130, 188-189
Hating your child   10
Heaven   46, 129, 167, 247, 259, 263
Hell   259,263
Helping Hand Jobs   226
Hobbies and interests   208, 234
Holidays   67-68
Hormones, teens   268
Horseplay   53   See also Wrestling, fighting
Hospitality   66, 241
House of love   See chapter 6; 52, 56, 59
Humanism   168, 261, 298
Ignoring   7, 20, 69, 115, 190, 227
Indecisive parent   38-40
Infanticide   130
Integrity   282
Intentional Parenting, definition   2, 17
Internet use and safety   231, 235, 268
Interrupting   189-190, 283
Introverts   69, 99
"It's all good" parent   42-43
Irresponsibility   190-191
Jealousy   53, 192-194
Job choices   295-297
Judgmental   194
Justice   130, 131, 216, 284
"Kind words only."   86
LGBT   270
Large families   104
Laziness   9, 138, 151, 195
Lazy parenting   10, 26-27
Learning Disabilities   141, 182

Learning styles   102
Legacy   4, 18, 64, 73, 90, 116, 316, 317
Lesbians   48, 270
Listening   57, 69, 70, 161, 181, 231, 283, 285, 287
Listening, how to   281-286
Life skills   chapter 17
Living counter-culturally   254-255
Living paradoxically   255-256
Living together (co-habitation)   43, 130, 303
Love languages   56-59, 209, 313
Lying   36, 38, 130, 153, 195-196
MKs (Missionaries' Kids)   165
Make-up   267, 278, 287
Making children mind   28, 81, 133
Marriage, preparation for   49-50, 60, 273-274, 298-303
Media   7, 44, 243, 269, 273, 288
Memories, making   65-68
Memorizing scripture   108, 253-254, Appendix 2
Mentoring   1, 67, 185
Mercy killing   130
Messiness   196-198
Mission trips, teens   209, 280
Modeling by adults   15, 16, 18, 24, 50, 60, 62, 80, 92, 106, 110, 156, 160, 184, 223, 245, 250, 265, 292
Moral absolutes   42-43, 130, 286
Motivation in parenting   167
Mouth washing   153

Movie choices 22, 35, 160, 176, 208, 255, 271, 273, 288, 309
Multiple punishments 155
Music choices 90, 165, 219, 253, 255, 287
Name-calling 36, 53, 63, 168
Narcissist 120-122, 208
Narcissistic parenting 27
Natural bent 95
Natural consequences 44, 152
Negativity 185, 200
Nursery, church 258-259
Nurturing 67, 73, 98, 149, 155; by fathers 61
Obedience 5, 15, 20-21, 76, 90; Chapter 13 (pp. 133-141); 157, 159, 161, 165, 227, 248, 252, 259
Obedience, quickly & quietly 21, 162
Opposite, practice 87, 122, 142, 145, 148, 151-152, 168
PKs (Preacher's Kids) 165
PMS 84, 156, 188
Parental posture, teen years 265-266, 305
Passages Museum 126
Passive wives 49, 60
Passivity 198, 205
Perfectionism 32, 54, 194, 205
Permissive parenting 8, 22-24
Personal devotions 251
People-pleasing, Fear of Man 199-200, 205
Personal boundaries 30, 40, 44, 47, 80, 123, 300, 307
Personality types 95, 98-100, 163, 164, 236, 237, 267
Pessimism 200

Physical goals 96-97
Physical touch and closeness 56
Picky eaters 201-203
Pornography 268-269
Pouting 204-205
Procrastination 205
Praise (affirmation) 21, 33, 101, 145, 159, 274
Prayer 49, 65, 95, 105, 107, 147, 221, 248, 253, 254, 302
Premarital counseling 301-302
Preparation for college 103, 280, 281, 297-298, 304, 309
Preparation for marriage 60, 72-73, 298-303
Pride 9, 111, 168, 203-204, 210
Principle-centered 3, 8, 24, 37, 221, 223, 248, 286-287, 313
Privileges 143, 147, 177
Prodigals 311-316
Promiscuity 48
Punctuality, lack of 207
Quality time 6, 25, 57
Quickly & quietly 21, 162, 227
RAD (Reactive Attachment Disorder) 207
Rage See Chapter 8; 7, 47, 48, 51, 82
Reactionary parent 41-42
Rebellion See Chapter 15(pp. 158-166), 205, 223, 249, 264, 286, 311
Rebellion, overt 161
Rebellion, subtle 161-162
Rebellion, teen 164, 293
Refuge, home as 64
Religions, other 129

Respect See Chapter 12 (pp. 115-132)
Respect for adults 115-116, 285
Respect for authority 91, 117-118
Respect for husband in marriage, unconditional 62-63
Respect for parents 74, 76, 115-116, 290; step-parents 76
Respect for peers & siblings 92, 119-120
Respect for property 122-124
Respect for things that belong to God 13, 18, 124-127
Respect for those who do not deserve respect 127-129
Respect, what not to 129-131
Respect while listening 283
Restitution 92, 122, 142, 148, 173, 212
Rewards 94, 110, 167, 202, 239, 259, 263; ticket system 177-179
Rudeness 208
Rule-Driven parent 36-38
Rules, consistency 77
Rules for family 91, 92, 97, 120, 122, 240, 288, 306
Rule of 3 (clothing) 232
Safe houses 47
Sacrifice in parenting 11, 120, 259
Salvation, children 246-247
Sarcasm 53, 284
Satan's lies, teens 276
Science 261-262

Secularism 7, 261-262
Selfishness 9, 120, 122, 173, 189, 208, 212 (see also narcissism)
Servant-leadership 61, 72
Sex 48, 72-73, 184, 220, 255, 287, 288, 303
Sex education 269-271, 304
Sharing 123
Sibling rivalry 120, 180, 209-210
Silent treatment 204-205
Single parents 73-75, 77, 104, 139
Sitting still, inability 93, 181, 210-211, 258-259
Skills list, by age 226-237
Skills, cooking 241-242
Social goals 96
Small groups 63, 67, 123
Small talk 95, 193, 234
Sneakiness 212
Spanking 11, 50, 147, 149-150, 205
Spiritual disciplines 248, 260
Spiritual gifting 103, 105
Spiritual goals 95
Spiritual life See Chapter 18 (pp. 245-263)
Stealing 19, 130, 173, 212
Stem cell research, embryonic 131
Step-parents 75
Steps in change 19
Strengths 49, 61, 95, 96, 99, 108, 203, 215, 236-237, 267, 300, 305, 316
Strong-willed child 11, 39, 51, 163, 264
Submission, wives' 48-50, 61, 73, 198

Suicide 7, 27, 43, 130, 291, 294-295
Suicide, assisted 130
TV tokens 243-244
Tag-team parenting 68-69, 74
Talents 95, 97, 121, 138, 192, 220, 237, 276-277
Tattling 190, 213
Tattoos 286
Teachable moments 256
Teen years See Chapter 20 (pp. 264-3040
Teen rebellion 164, 293
Temper Tantrums 16, 28, 87, 161, 172
Test Anxiety 234
Therapy see "Counseling"
Thinking analytically 237, 282
Threatening parent 20-21, 285, 294
Time management 182, 206, 207, 235
Time-outs 33, 151, 156
Tired child v. obedience 140-141, 218, 258
Trades, the 297
Training v. Control chart 135
Transition, teens to adulthood 277-281
Tunnel of Chaos 63-64, 237
Unbelieving spouses 79-80
Unconditional love for children 101
Unconditional love in marriage 61-62
Unforgiveness 35, 148, 211
Uniqueness 98, 105
Unity in parenting 14, 68
Unjust parenting 30-31, 155
Unprotective parent 35
Unsafe people 35, 271

Values 4-5, 7-9, 18, 24, 35-36, 103, 110, 215, 245, 255, 269-270, 275, 309, 313
Vanity 215-216
Vengeance 216-217
Venting 86
Voice tone 20, 284
Warning, in correction 81, 144, 150
Warning signs of suicide 295
Wastefulness 217
Weaknesses 95, 96, 108, 139, 203, 223, 236-237, 305
Whining 21, 161, 170, 172, 218-219, 227
Willfulness 6, 15, 131, 145, 158-159
Words of Affirmation 57, 314
Work ethic 90, 97
Worldliness 8, 22, 219-221
Worldview, Christian 90, 103, 262-263, 298, 304
Worry 221-222
Wrestling 222
Youth groups 259, 292-293

For additional copies of
Intentional Parenting

Send $21.95 plus $4 shipping and handling to:

>Axiom Press, LLC
>2910 N. Powers Blvd. #241
>Colorado Springs, CO 80922

Or visit our website at www.IntentionalParenting.us or call us at (719) 299-0814.

Discounts are available for 10 or more copies sent to a single address.

<u>Ship to:</u>
Name _____
Address_____
_____
City, State, Zip _____
Phone (in case of questions or problems)
_____
Email _____

____ Please do not add me to your mailing list
   (Your information will not be shared with others)